D0875200

THE HOLOCAUST LADY

THE HOLOCAUST LADY

RUTH MINSKY SENDER

MACMILLAN PUBLISHING COMPANY   NEW YORK

MAXWELL MACMILLAN CANADA   TORONTO

MAXWELL MACMILLAN INTERNATIONAL
NEW YORK   OXFORD   SINGAPORE   SYDNEY

Macmillan Publishing Company is part of the
Maxwell Communication Group of Companies.
Macmillan Publishing Company
866 Third Avenue, New York, NY 10022
Maxwell Macmillan Canada, Inc.
1200 Eglinton Avenue East, Suite 200
Don Mills, Ontario M3C 3N1
First edition
Printed in the United States of America
10   9   8   7   6   5   4   3   2   1

The text of this book is set in 13 point Garamond No. 3.

Library of Congress Cataloging-in-Publication Data
Sender, Ruth Minsky.
The Holocaust lady / Ruth Minsky Sender. — 1st ed.
p.   cm.
Summary: In an effort to teach children about the Holocaust,
the author describes the impact of this horrifying event on
her life and the lives of other survivors.
ISBN 0-02-781832-2
1. Sender, Ruth Minsky—Juvenile literature.   2. Holocaust
survivors—United States—Biography—Juvenile literature.   3. Jews—
United States—Biography—Juvenile literature.   4. Holocaust,
Jewish (1939–1945)—Study and teaching—United States—Juvenile
literature.   [1. Sender, Ruth Minsky.   2. Holocaust survivors.
3. Jews—Biography.   4. Holocaust, Jewish (1939–1945)]   I. Title.
D804.3.S448   1992   940.53'18—dc20   92-13268

To all those who perished but are not forgotten,
a memorial

To all those who found the courage to go on,
a tribute

To my children and grandchildren for remaining
compassionate, warm human beings,
my gratitude and love

To Beverly for her sensitivity as editor of
The Cage, To Life, The Holocaust Lady,
thank you

THE HOLOCAUST LADY

1

The long, hushed hallways stretch before me in many directions. Slowly, carefully, I check the numbers on the classroom doors. I want room forty-one.

Through the open doors, I see young children busy at work. Free. Safe. Secure. I stop and stare silently. Lucky, lucky children. How we take freedom for granted.

Two young girls appear in the hall, chatting happily. They are about ten years old. One is blond, with long hair falling over her shoulders. The other has curly dark hair that encircles her head like a crown. They smile politely as they come closer.

"Hello, girls. Can you help me, please?"

"Are you lost in our school?" The dark-haired girl studies my face with open curiosity. "What are you looking for?" Her voice is soft.

"Room forty-one." I smile.

"Did you come to see the Holocaust Lady?" There is sudden excitement in her voice.

"You mean to *hear* the Holocaust Lady." The other corrects her quickly.

I feel a sharp pain in my chest. My new title catches me by surprise. My voice trembles. "I am 'the Holocaust Lady.' "

They stare, bewildered. "You are?" they say together.

A picture of a bag lady I saw once at a train station flashes through my mind. I stared at her in the same way. She carried two heavy bags. Her life, her past, she carried in those bags.

I, too, carry heavy bags. Invisible bags. Bags filled with memories of horror, pain, courage, hope. My life. My past.

Each time I open my bags, the memories come to life. The people who died appear to plead, to demand, *Speak for us.* Children—blue-eyed, brown-eyed, dark, fair, young and innocent, much like the children before me—whisper, *Tell them about us. Tell them how we lived. Tell them how we hoped. Tell them how we died.*

"Yes, I am the Holocaust Lady." My voice sounds strange. "I am the Holocaust Lady."

I take their warm hands in mine. It feels good. Hand in hand, we walk into room forty-one.

A young woman, smiling warmly, moves quickly toward me, her hand outstretched in greeting. "You must be Mrs. Sender." She holds my hand tightly. "I'm Mrs. Warfield. I'm so glad you accepted the invitation to speak to us."

She turns toward the class. "Children, please say hello to Mrs. Ruth Minsky Sender, the author of *The Cage* and *To Life.*"

All eyes are on me. "Hello, Mrs. Sender. Welcome."

On the teacher's desk I see copies of *The Cage,* my first book. It feels wonderful seeing my book in a classroom. Children and adults will read it and learn of my world, the world that was destroyed, the world we must not forget.

I hear the teacher's soft voice. "We are all so eager to read *The Cage.* We would like you to autograph the books for us, Mrs. Sender."

Mrs. Warfield's voice is music to my ears.

"I spoke to the children about you. We read together your piece in the *New York Times.* They are overwhelmed by your experiences, and very, very proud to meet you."

I swallow the lump in my throat as I move to the front of the classroom. "My name is Ruth Minsky Sender. I am a Holocaust survivor."

The children's eyes wander, bewildered, from my light-brown hair, falling in soft curls, to my neat blue pin-striped suit and pale blue blouse. Silently their eyes search for traces of the shaved head, the sunken cheeks, the rags, the concentration camp number. I see the puzzled look I have met many times before: She looks normal.

"I do not look any different now than your mothers, grandmothers, teachers. I am a mother, grandmother, teacher, writer. Still"—I swallow hard—"I am very different. I am a Holocaust survivor." I move closer to the wide-eyed children before me and take a deep breath. "As a Holocaust survivor I carry a heavy burden, a painful

11

duty. The burden of remembering. The duty of passing on the agonizing memories so that the world will learn from them. It should not happen again. It cannot happen again."

Not a sound is heard. All eyes are glued to my face. My voice quivers. "I am here to share the horrors of human degradation. I am here to share the acts of courage, of spiritual resistance against evil."

My voice is stronger now. "No matter how hard it is, I, the survivor, make you, too, witnesses. Together we take on the painful duty of remembering, the awesome task of standing guard against indifference, against prejudice, against injustice."

I see the children's intense stares, and pictures of cattle cars flash before my eyes. Cattle cars filled with men, women, children. Their eyes wide with horror, confusion, disbelief.

I see the terrified eyes of my younger brothers, Motele, sixteen, Moishele, thirteen, as we enter the gates of hell, Auschwitz. Their last, desperate words echo in my ears: *Riva, we must live. We must survive.* In the stillness of the classroom, they call to me, *Remember! Remember! You survived. It is your duty to bear witness.*

I raise my voice. "Each Holocaust survivor, each liberator of the Nazi death camps has the duty to bear witness."

I have an overwhelming urge to take all the children

here into my arms and hold them close, shield them from evil. My mind races from the past to the present, from the present to the past. I hear tormented voices. Children who never grew up cry, *We want to live. We want to live.*

The somber eyes of the children in the room ask silently, How could this happen? Could it happen again?

My hands tremble as I pick up from the desk a journal I carry with me. "This journal, published by a hate group in America, dares to deny that millions of innocent men, women, and children were all murdered by the Nazis." I feel overwhelming outrage. "They try to tell me that the horrors I witnessed never happened. They try to tell me that my family never lived. They try to tell me that there was no Holocaust. They spread their ugly lies while there are still survivors to bear witness to the truth.

"What will happen when the survivors and the liberators are gone? You, my dear children, will have to be witnesses. You will stand guard against hatred and indifference."

I stop to catch my breath. "I saw how people close to me were taught to hate." I remember the smiling face of my childhood friend, blond, blue-eyed Harry.

"I was thirteen years old when the Nazis marched into Lodz, a huge industrial city in Poland. I grew up in a Jewish working-class neighborhood that later became part of the ghetto. I had two sisters and four brothers.

"My best friend, Harry, was an only child and spent

most of his time at our home. His grandmother, Mrs. Gruber, and his mother, Olga, were close friends of our family. They were of German descent. We were Jews. We shared each other's holidays. Shared joy and sorrow. They spoke Yiddish, as did all the people in that neighborhood; they knew Jewish history and Jewish customs. We were all one family.

"When the Nazis invaded Poland, they proclaimed that everyone with Jewish ancestors, even if they had converted to Christianity, was a Jew; they must wear the yellow Star of David and vacate homes outside the area designated for Jews. Everyone with German ancestors, they said, was now a *Volksdeutsche,* a German. Theirs was the power of life and death.

"Within three months, our best friends changed. They moved to the best section of the city of Lodz. They took whatever they wanted from their Jewish friends and neighbors.

"One day Harry came to see us, dressed in the brown uniform of the Hitler Youth, a nightstick in his hand. His big, blue eyes were strangely cold. From his mouth rushed the same hate words we heard all day long on the Nazi radio. I was horrified.

" 'Harry, you were my friend, you were my brother, you grew up among Jews. How can you repeat that ugly propaganda?'

"For a moment, only a moment, he looked a little

ashamed. Then a Harry I'd never known, in a voice I'd never heard, replied, 'Germany is my fatherland. I'll do anything for my fatherland.'

"I found out after liberation that Harry had been killed on a German front. I cried for him. I cried for myself."

My voice cracks. "If people like Harry, Mrs. Gruber, and Olga could be brainwashed, could be taught to hate the people they knew, respected, and loved, you can imagine what hatred can do, what indifference can do. My mother, a strong believer in social justice and brotherhood, insisted, 'A world full of people will not be silent.' "

I feel tears grasping my throat. The students wait in silence. "She was wrong. The world she trusted was indifferent. Silent. She perished. She was taken out of the ghetto during a Nazi raid on September 10, 1942. I never saw her again. She became a statistic.

"But I held on to hope that she was alive. That hope helped me survive." Tears flow over my face. I wipe them quickly. "When I returned to Lodz from the death camps, I learned that the people taken from Lodz in September 1942 were gassed in trucks in the town of Chelmno. The trucks had Red Cross symbols on them. The people entering them believed that they were going to be examined by doctors, but gas was pumped into the trucks. They all died. My mother was one of them."

I stop to compose myself. "If you happen to see the

documentary *Shoah,* take note of the scene with the quiet, green fields in Chelmno. Numbers slide across the screen, numbers of those murdered there. When you see those numbers, remember, they were people. Think of them as people, not numbers. Think of my mother, a loving, compassionate woman who believed in a world that would not be silent."

Now I see tears in some of the children's eyes. "In my mother's words, 'As long as there is life, there is hope.'

"Never give up hope. We held on to hope surrounded by death. We fought moral decay by teaching values. We hid books and studied secretly. We held on to life. It took courage. It took strength."

My mother, my brothers appear before my eyes and vanish just as quickly. They died. I survived—and became "the Holocaust Lady."

2

I glance at the clock. It has been over an hour since I began sharing my past with the eager listeners before me. Silently they have journeyed with me through secret study groups, hidden libraries. They have tried to imagine what it was like to feel the pain of hunger, to find the strength to make a small bread ration last for a whole week, to water down a bowl of soup so that it could be shared with three starving little brothers.

"I was sixteen years old when the Nazis took my mother from us." I see the wagon, the ghetto policeman keeping Mama from jumping off. "My brother Laibele was dying from tuberculosis. I suddenly became the mother of three younger children. They were about the same ages some of you are.

"We held on to one another. When I became sick from malnutrition, they sold the bread rations that were to last for a week to get some vitamins for me on the black market. That took physical strength. That took love and devotion."

A child in the front row wipes her tears. My eyes pause on her. "We all have hidden strength that helps us even when all seems hopeless."

Her eyes meet mine. There is a sudden glow of relief in them.

I continue. "I wrote poetry on scraps of paper in the Nazi concentration camps. The other girls stole pieces of paper from the wastebaskets at the factories where we performed slave labor, hid the paper on their bodies, and gave it to me to write on. I wrote poems of hope. Poems of anger. That was spiritual resistance."

Suddenly a boy raises his hand. "Did you ever find your brothers again?"

I bite my lip. "No. I saw them the last time on August 27, 1944, at the gates of Auschwitz. But I still live with the hope that maybe, somehow, they survived. I did. . . ."

My voice quivers. "This is the tragedy of the survivors. False hope. We have no graves. It is always a tragedy when loved ones die. Still, most people have a grave to go to, a marker with a name. They scream. They cry. They are angry. They know the person in that grave will never return to them. There is no false hope. They have memories, pictures of the life they shared together."

I stop. I try to recall the faces of my loved ones. They are a blur. "We have no pictures of our families, only blurred images that come and go.

"I still write to organizations that help search for survivors. The answer is always the same: No trace. Yet I hope for a miracle.

"Sometimes miracles do happen. In Miami, Florida, not long ago, people stood in line to get into a famous restaurant. The line was very long. A man, speaking Yiddish, turned to his wife and said, 'This is crazy, to stay in line for food. We are not starving.'

" 'For this restaurant, the wait is worth it,' another man standing nearby said. He, too, spoke Yiddish.

"They began a casual conversation. 'Your Yiddish dialect seems to be from Poland,' the man said.

" 'Yes. I am from Lodz,' answered the other.

" 'I, too, am from Lodz.'

" 'Oh, yes? Where from Lodz?'

"And the miracle that survivors dream of happened. They discovered that they are cousins. Both were children when they were sent to Nazi concentration camps. Each one thought that the other had not survived. But they both had survived. And then, after so many years, they met by accident.

"I gain hope from such rare miracles. I faced death many times. Still I am here. Motele and Moishele were young. Maybe . . . somehow . . ." My voice trails off.

"Did the Holocaust change your life?" a girl asks softly.

I search for the right words. I feel the lump in my throat again. "If you wake up screaming at night so many years after the Holocaust. . . . Yes, it changed my life forever. The survivors will always live with the agony of the past."

Hands keep popping up. "Would you ever go back to Poland? Germany?"

"No. No. No. There is nothing for me there anymore."

"When did you come to America?"

"February 2, 1950. After eleven years of horror, pain, and degradation. Years of being caged in a ghetto, in Nazi death camps and labor camps, then of being in

19

displaced persons camps. On February 2, 1950, I found a home at last."

My mind wanders back to that day.

3

"Is this really America, Mommy? Really?"

The voice of my three-year-old son, Laibele, rings with joy. The Statue of Liberty glistens in the early morning sun, calling to us, the lonely survivors of the Holocaust: Welcome to the shores of freedom.

"Yes, this is America. Finally we are here." I hug him tightly. The hard, long boat journey is suddenly forgotten. The uncertainty and despair have turned to hope.

Jovial voices fill the air.

"We are in America."

"Life is waiting for us."

"We survived."

"We are in America."

Tears of joy, tears of sorrow flow over my face. I survived. I am in America at last. But my mother, my brothers. Why did they die? Why? Why? Why? I hold my smiling little boy close. Our joy will always be woven with pain.

Our names are called. "Moishe Senderowicz. Ruta Senderowicz. Laibl Senderowicz. Avrom Senderowicz."

My heart pounds as we are guided off the boat by an American immigration official. I am on American soil. I am in America.

Laibele clutches my hand. My seven-month-old baby boy, Avromele, sleeps soundly in his father's arms.

We are led into a huge, open waiting area. People rush about, searching for someone to welcome them. I hear agitated, tense voices as people meet for the first time, then joyous greetings, loud sobs. Unspoken questions hang heavily in the air. Eyes filled with sorrow give unspoken answers: No one else survived.

I feel lost, nervous. A stranger in a big, new land.

"You wait here." The immigration official points to an empty bench. "A representative of the Hebrew Immigration Aid Society will meet you soon and put you on a train to Boston, where your sponsor is waiting for you." He quickly moves on.

Our sponsor, Morris Borenstein, Moniek's uncle, lives in Malden, Massachusetts. Our ship, the USAT *General A. W. Greely,* docked in New York harbor. We stare at one another, bewildered, as we put our bundles on the floor. We are here. We must have patience.

I study the faces of the people around me. Nervous. Frightened. Hopeful. I hear many voices. Many languages fill the air with strange sounds. A group of people speak in English.

"Why do they talk so fast, Mommy?" Laibele asks.

"It sounds to me as if they have hot potatoes in their mouths and have to keep talking so they won't get burned, Laibele."

"You are funny, Mommy. Will I learn to speak like that?"

I put my arm around my son. "Children learn fast, Laibele. I wonder how our Yiddish sounds to them."

"Like we have hot potatoes in our mouths?" Laibele laughs.

His laughter puts me more at ease.

He plays with his paper boat as he watches the people rushing about. "I am hungry, Mommy. Can I have something to eat?"

"I have nothing to give you." I feel a sharp pain in my chest. My child is hungry and I have no food for him.

How often did I hear the words "I am hungry" from my little brothers in the ghetto. I still feel the pain, the frustration, the anger. But now I am free. I am in America. My child must not go hungry.

I take him by the hand. "Come, darling, we will find a place that sells food. We have some American money. Come."

The waiting area around us is less crowded now. Many of the new arrivals have already left. At one corner a group of people stands around a wooden counter, speaking English. We walk closer. There is a glass showcase in front of the counter. It is filled with small packages wrapped in white paper. The man behind the counter turns toward me. He speaks English. I do not understand what he is saying. I only know a few English words. "Bread. Salami."

I hold out a ten-dollar bill that had been given to us by the immigration officials before we left Germany. "You must have some money when you enter the country," they had said.

"Bread. Salami," I repeat slowly.

The man shakes his head. "No bread. No salami."

He tries to explain something, but I do not understand him. I feel helpless. My child is hungry. I stare at the people around me. If only I could communicate with them, maybe they could help. I try speaking Yiddish, Polish, German. They do not understand. Tears well up in my eyes. My child is hungry in America . . . in America. . . .

Someone buys one of the white packages. He sits down on a bench nearby. Slowly he opens the package and takes out two slices of bread with something in between. I smell salami.

Quickly I turn back to the counter, hold up three fingers, and point at the white packages in the showcase. The man behind the counter hands me three packages, takes the ten dollars from my outstretched hand, gives me some change. He looks embarrassed as he tries to explain something to me that I do not understand.

Treasures in hand, we rush back to Moniek. My child is not hungry anymore.

After a long wait, a man approaches. He looks flushed, upset. "You must be the Senderowicz family. Welcome to America." He extends his hand in greeting, speaking Yiddish. "I am from the Hebrew Immigration Aid Society. I should have been here several hours ago. I was given the wrong time for your arrival. I am so sorry you had to sit here alone. You must have felt abandoned. Did you have any problems?"

The sound of Yiddish, the ability to communicate, the warmth of this stranger, ready to help, overwhelms me. "Well." My voice betrays my frustration. "I tried to buy bread and salami to feed my hungry child from the man at the stand over there, but he did not understand me and shook his head. When I saw that the little packages he is selling have salami and bread, I pointed, and he sold them to me. Why didn't he sell them to me when I asked for bread and salami? Why do they sell it sliced and in packages?"

His lips form a soft smile. "You have just learned an American custom. Those are sandwiches. They are wrapped in waxed paper to keep fresh. In waiting rooms, they do not sell bread and salami in chunks, they sell it in sandwiches. I am sure that is what the man tried to explain to you."

"Sandwiches," I repeat slowly. Sandwiches. A new English word. A new custom. An American custom.

"Welcome to America." He picks up our bundles. "I'll put you on a train to Boston. Your uncle and your cousins will be waiting at the station. I am glad you are here at last."

I see tears in his eyes.

4

My heart pounds as we enter the train. Pictures of cattle cars crammed with people flash through my mind. I take a deep breath. I am in America. I am free.

Laibele's eyes dance curiously from one passenger to the other. "They do not look any different than we do," he mumbles softly. "They speak different, but do not look different."

I hold him close. "I wonder if they think the same about us."

The baby, his fingers curled around his father's thumb, sleeps peacefully. My eyes glance lovingly over the faces of my little family.

Moniek's eyes have a faraway look. "It is so strange. An uncle, cousins, waiting for me. Family I only know from letters and pictures." His voice is low. "I hope they have some pictures of my mother, father, and brothers." He stares at the passing scenery. "I wish I could recall the faces of my family. They appear, then quickly vanish. Why can't I remember them clearly?"

My eyes well up with tears. I, too, try to recall the face of my mother, her smile, the twinkle of my brothers' eyes. If only we had pictures. If . . . if . . . if . . .

My mind wanders back to May 1945. I am standing alone at the door of my former home. I have survived the death camps. I am back. I am free.

I have returned to search for pictures of my family. But the home I shared with my brothers Motele and Moishele is not my home any longer.

A Polish woman stands in the doorway. "What do you want here? This is my home now. The Jewish homes were given to us Poles." Why did you survive? her angry look demands.

"I came for pictures of my family. I only want pictures."

"I have no pictures! I threw them out with the books I found here!" she shouts. "I threw them all in the garbage in the backyard!"

The books of our secret library, which we risked our lives for, the pictures, the only traces of my family, she

26

threw in the garbage. I shiver as I search the garbage: broken pieces of furniture, torn books, broken glass. No pictures.

"If only we had pictures," I whisper hoarsely as I take Moniek's hand in mine. "If only we had pictures."

A woman and a young girl walk by slowly. The girl is about ten years old, with long brown hair. They smile at us. I smile. I try to recall what I looked like when I was ten. I cannot.

A line from a poem I learned in school pops suddenly into my head. "Freedom is like good health. We value it only when we have lost it." I study the faces of the passengers around me. Do they value their freedom? Do they take for granted having family, looking at pictures?

5

"Boston! Boston!" calls the train conductor. "Boston!"

"We are here, Laibele." I gently nudge my sleeping little boy. "We are here."

"We are in Boston!" He is wide awake now. "We are in Boston!"

I feel apprehensive as we make our way toward the train door. Is Moniek's family at the station? Will they recognize us from the picture we sent them? Will they be happy to meet us?

I glance at Moniek. His eyes are tense. He, too, is wondering.

As we step onto the station platform, a short, elderly man rushes toward us, his face radiant. "Moishe Senderowicz. I am your uncle, Morris Borenstein." He puts his arms tightly around Moniek. "I would know you anyplace." He speaks Yiddish. "You look like Chava, your mother." His voice cracks. "If only your mother's sister, my dear Etta, had lived to see this day." He wipes the tears from his face. "You are the only survivor from the family we left behind in Poland. The only survivor."

I hear introductions. I feel warm embraces. My eyes overflow with tears of happiness. We are not alone anymore.

We are driven to our uncle's home in Malden. More cousins and their families are waiting to greet their newfound relatives. The sound of their voices says welcome. The glow of their eyes says welcome. The warm touch of their hands says welcome.

Laibele sits on the floor, surrounded by children. They speak English. He speaks Yiddish. I watch him nervously. The children are showing him toys. They smile at him. He smiles at them. One of the children takes a little car, pushes it forward. Laibele takes a little car, pushes it forward. They are communicating. I hear the happy laughter of children at play.

It is strange to be inside a real home again. In the long years of passing from concentration camp to concentration camp, then, after liberation, from displaced persons camp to displaced persons camp, I have forgotten what a home looks like. This house—spacious, warm, comfortable—amazes me. It is so new, so wonderful.

I stare at a mysterious white enamel box. It has two doors. They are opened and closed often. Inside the box are put butter, milk, cheese, meats. Why do these people put perishable foods inside a box? In Europe we put those foods on ice.

Moniek's cousin Minnie notices my horrified look.

"Ruth, what is the matter?" she says in Yiddish.

"All that food will spoil. You will have to throw it out. You must not throw out food." My voice is tight.

"Come." She takes me by the hand, walks up to the mysterious box, opens the door. A surge of cold air rushes at me. I move back.

"This is an electric icebox, Ruth. A refrigerator."

"A refrigerator," I repeat, fascinated by the wonder of an electric icebox. "A refrigerator."

Minnie smiles. "See, there is nothing to worry about. Eat. Eat."

She walks me to the table, laden with breads, cheeses, pastries. "Eat. Eat."

I see the hungry eyes of my little brothers, Motele, Laibele, Moishele. I hear Laibele's voice. *Someday we will all be together at a table filled with bread, and we'll eat, eat, eat until we can eat no more.*

I wipe my tears quickly. No one asks questions. I feel their compassion, warmth, sensitivity, and I am grateful for their silence.

I stare at the large, white loaves of bread before me and remember a small, dark lump of bread. Our weekly bread ration in the ghetto. I see Motele, carefully slicing the claylike bread. *We must make it last for a whole week. Those who eat it all at once—and it would not take much to eat it—die much sooner.*

On the table now, fresh white bread calls, Eat. Eat. Eat. No rations. Eat. I reach for the bread, but my hand stops in midair. I see Moishele's famished eyes. I remember his wish: to sit near a table laden with bread and not feel hungry anymore.

Our new-found family is leaving, saying their good-byes. Cousin Yiddl shakes hands with Moniek. I watch them. First cousins. They both look like their mothers, who were sisters. Yet each one's childhood, each one's youth, was so different.

"See you later," Yiddl says warmly, in English, as he and his family part with us.

"See you later," I repeat slowly.

Minnie, who with her family shares the house with Uncle, cleans the tables. I start to help.

"No, no. You had a long, hard day. An emotional day. You go upstairs and go to sleep."

"We cannot go to sleep yet, Minnie. We have to wait for Yiddl."

"Why?" She looks puzzled.

"Well, he said, 'See you later.' That means he is coming back soon."

"No. That's another way of saying good-bye."

"Oh," I mumble. "I feel foolish."

"Don't feel foolish. You'll soon learn English."

"My first day in America, and already I have learned about sandwiches, refrigerators, a new way of saying good-bye, and not to translate every word or expression literally."

"You will be all right." She smiles.

"Is *all right* the same as *okay?*" I ask quickly.

"Yes. You are learning fast. Now, go to bed!"

The bedroom is warm and cozy. The baby is sleeping in a crib near our bed. Laibele is in a bed in the next room.

It has been six weeks since we slept together in a real bed. At Bremen, the port of departure in Germany, we slept on cots in different buildings, men in one, women and children in the other. On the boat the men and women were on different decks on cots.

It feels good to have a real bed. I move close to Moniek. "Is it real? Are we finally here? Are we really in America, or am I dreaming?"

He puts his arms around me. "It does feel like a dream."

6

"Sender—Sender—Sen-der-o-wicz." The clerk at the Immigration and Naturalization office struggles to pronounce our last name. We are here to file applications for American citizenship. If all goes well and we prove ourselves qualified, pass written tests and oral tests, we will become American citizens in five years. Five years of waiting. Again, waiting.

My thoughts race quickly. Could they still send us back? I shiver.

"How do you spell *Sen-der-o-wicz?*"

"Spell means to sound out," I remember a young man in the displaced persons camp, who knew some English, telling me.

"S-e-n-d-e-r-o-w-i-c-z." I try to sound out the letters slowly, carefully.

My Polish pronunciation is hard for the clerk to understand. She looks confused "S-e-n-d-e-r," she repeats slowly, then stops. "S-e-n-d-e-r, S-e-n-d-e-r- what?"

"S-e-n-d-e-r-o-w-i-c-z. S-e-n-d-e-r-o-w-i-c-z," I say very slowly.

"S-e-n-d-e-r—" She sounds frustrated. "S-e-n-d-e-r—"

"You have a hard and long name." Speaking Yiddish, a middle-aged woman looks up from her desk. "You will have problems every time you are asked to spell your name. You should shorten your name and make it easier on yourselves."

Moniek looks upset. "My name is Senderowicz. What is so hard about it?"

"It may be easy for you. But your accent and your long name will make it hard for others. You will run into problems."

"We had enough problems. We do not need any more." He sighs heavily. "But if I change my name, how will they find me?" He bites his lip. "If people are searching for me, how will they find me?"

"If—if—if" Her voice breaks. She takes a deep breath. "If they survived, they will find you. You are not changing your name. You are only shortening it." She speaks softly. "Make it easier for your children. You will have to give them American names. Their Yiddish names will sound funny to other children. Make it easier for your children."

33

I look at Moniek. "We came to America to find a home for our children, an easier life for them."

She takes my hand in hers. "Laibele could be Louis. Avromele, Allen. You are not taking away their Yiddish names. You are adding American names." Her voice is warm. "I know how you feel about their Yiddish names. They are the names of people you loved, people who died, people who live on only in their names."

Only in their names echoes in my ears as I see myself again in Lodz, my former home, searching for family in 1945. I pass Shrudmienska Street. My heart skips a beat. My uncle Baruch, his wife, Eva, and their baby, Rutka, once lived here. He was a prominent educator, she a successful bookkeeper. Their baby, Rutka, was the joy of their life. I spent many happy times playing with, cuddling the beautiful little girl.

When the Nazis came, Uncle Baruch, Aunt Eva, and Rutka smuggled their way into Russia. Later the Nazis attacked Russia. My beloved uncle, my charming aunt, my darling little cousin perished. Not a trace is left of that beautiful family.

I stop, stare at the street where many Jewish families once made their homes. They all vanished. I try to recall Rutka's happy laughter, the sound of her childish voice as she walked to the park, securely holding her mother's and father's hands. The sound, like the child, cannot be brought back.

I wipe tears from my face. I'll make her name live on by calling myself Ruth, the mature form of Rutka. Riva, Ruth. The initial will still be the same. "The names live on," I whisper softly. "Senderowicz, Sender. Laibele, Louis. Avromele, Allen. Riva, Ruth." I smile. "What about Moishe?"

"Well, Moishe is Morris," says the woman.

I turn to my husband. "To me you will always be Moniek. No matter how our names change, we will still be the same. If the changes will make our children Americanized, if it will make their lives easier. . . ."

"Senderowicz. Sender. S-e-n-d-e-r," Moniek repeats hoarsely. "If it will help our children. . . ."

"Sender!" the immigration clerk calls out, pleased. "Sender. This I can spell."

7

In a displaced persons camp, at a school sponsored by the Organization for Rehabilitation through Training, Moniek had learned woodworking. Uncle finds him a job as a carpenter. The work is hard, the wages small. "I cannot support my family," Moniek laments. "I must find other work. I do not want to be a burden to anyone. Uncle is good to us; we have a roof over our heads. But we must find an apartment of our own. I must earn more money."

Finally he finds a better-paying job in a meat-packing plant, making frankfurters. At night he learns English at the Malden high school. I study on my own at home while the children are asleep.

We move to an apartment at 12 Lime Street in Malden. It is an old house, with a coal-burning furnace, a fenced-in backyard, and a cherry tree. Laibele is overjoyed. A tree. A cherry tree.

I watch my child running happily around the tree, and my mind fills with visions of my childhood in Lodz. I see the tired eyes of our neighbors, their hard struggle to make a living written on their faces, gathering around the huge old oak tree in our yard.

"Such a beautiful tree."

"A *mechaye*." A delight.

"I dream all winter of that tree, its branches, its peaceful shade."

"Somehow under the strong branches of this oak tree, life seems brighter."

"The future is full of promise."

Tears choke me. Little did we know that we had no future. The tree was chopped up for firewood in the ghetto to keep us from freezing to death. My neighbors died in Nazi death camps.

I stare at the blossoming tree in my new home in a free

country, and hear the voices of my old home, the voices of my vanished world.

"I am Carl, your neighbor," I hear someone call from the other side of the fence.

I look up, startled back to the present. A black man in his forties smiles broadly at me.

"May I come over?"

"Please do," I reply, opening the gate.

"I saw your little boy playing in the yard, and your baby sleeping in the carriage." He lowers his voice in order not to wake the baby. "I love children." He smiles at Laibele. "My brother and I, two old bachelors, have been sharing this house for many years. We were so happy to see young people with children move in next door."

His voice is warm, his manner gentle. He extends his hand in greeting. "What part of Europe are you from?"

I stare at him, surprised. "How did you know I am from Europe?"

"Your accent." He laughs.

"Oh." I feel myself blush. "I forgot."

"Are you from Poland or Germany?"

"I am a Jew who happened to be born in Poland."

He stares at the cloudless blue sky for a long, silent moment. "Were you in the Nazi concentration camps?"

"Yes." My voice cracks.

"I'm sorry. I didn't mean to bring back painful memories."

He takes my hand in his, holds it for a moment. "I read about the horrors. I saw pictures of the death camps- . . . .But when you meet someone who was there . . . it becomes real. . . ."

How do I tell him how real it is? How do I tell him of the nightmare I live with? I remain silent.

My baby, sleeping peacefully in the carriage next to me, stirs softly. I lift him into my arms, hold him tight.

The past is real.

The present is real.

8

Our other neighbors, Jack and Berta, come to meet us one day. She seems to be in her late thirties, he a little older. "We came to welcome you to America." Jack extends his hand.

Berta's eyes look longingly at the baby as she shakes my hand. "It is nice to have children. We are not that blessed."

I feel her sadness, her emptiness. Suddenly I smell the smoke-filled air of Auschwitz again, the stench of burning flesh. I hear the piercing screams of children being torn away from their mothers.

They took my children from me. The voice of my friend Tola rings in my ears. *They took my children. How can I go on living?* Tola survived. Where did she find the strength?

Mama's tear-stained face flashes before me as she tries to comfort her friend Balchia, whose children were taken during a Nazi raid in the ghetto of Lodz. "Balchia, you have to be strong. You must live."

They cry in each other's arms. Her head bowed low, Balchia drags herself toward her empty home. Mama, tears pouring over her face, whispers hoarsely, "I could not live without my children."

Mothers without children. Children without mothers. How did they go on?

Tears glide silently over my cheeks.

"My heart goes out to the survivors of the Holocaust." Jack's voice cracks. "They suffered so much. . . ." He turns his eyes toward the window. "Berta and I are Jews." He looks at Berta. "There but for the grace of God go we."

"I would never have the strength to survive." Berta wipes her eyes.

"Berta." I take a deep breath. "Berta, you do not know how strong you can be, until put to the test. Heroes or cowards are not born that way. They are created by circumstances."

"What gave *you* the strength to live?" Berta's voice is very low.

"What gave me the strength to live," I repeat slowly as my thoughts wander back to the death camps again. "Hope. Hope that my family would survive. Hope gave me the strength to hold on to life."

I raise my voice. "Hope. Anger. A duty to bear witness. Hunger for revenge. All these helped us survive."

Jack turns suddenly toward me. "Did you take revenge?"

"No." My voice quivers. "When the day of liberation finally came, we could not. . . . It was not in us. All we wanted was to rush back to what once were our homes, hoping to find someone alive." I swallow hard. "No. We did not take revenge."

I look at Laibele running happily in the yard, Avromele peacefully cooing. "We survived. We rose from the ashes, built a new life. . . . This is our revenge."

"What about the murderers of our people? They must pay," Jack's voice thunders.

"Our murderers must account for their evil deeds. I hope all of them will be caught. Stand trial. Be judged by the world. Pay for their crimes. I hope the world learns from the past."

We stare at one another in painful silence.

9

"I have wonderful news, Lillie! Wonderful news! My sisters, Mala and Chana, and their families are at last leaving the displaced persons camp in Germany."

Lillie, Moniek's cousin, smiles through her tears as she sits near me at the kitchen table. "Ruth, it is wonderful to see you so happy. All the years of separation, then finding one another, only to be separated again. Now it is finally coming to an end. The wandering will soon be over."

"The wandering will soon be over." I repeat Lillie's words slowly. "It will soon be over. I was only thirteen when my sisters, Mala and Chana, and my brother Yankl smuggled their way over the Russian border to escape the Nazis. They were the older children in our family of seven.

"My mother, a widow, remained with her four little ones in Poland. She did not feel that we were in any danger. 'Who would harm a widow? Who would harm young children?' she would say. If only we had known we, too, would have left Poland. My mother, my little brothers would have survived."

I take a deep breath. "Even if we had been told what

evil awaited us, we would never have believed it. How could anyone believe such things?"

Lillie touches my hand gently.

"I was twenty when my sisters, my brother, and I found one another again in the displaced persons camps, in Germany. I was the only one left." I swallow hard. "Very few survivors found family."

Lillie listens silently.

"Five years we went from one displaced persons camp to another, waiting to be rescued again. We were lucky. Your father sent us visas to America. He sponsored Moniek, me, and the children. I said good-bye to my sisters and brother, not knowing if I would see them again."

A smile brightens my face. "Lillie, miracles do happen. Mala, Yosef, and their children, Abramek and Esther received visas to America through HIAS, the Hebrew Immigration Aid Society. They will leave soon and arrive in Boston Harbor, then take the train from Boston to New York. My brother Yankl left the displaced persons camp in Germany for Canada earlier. He got a visa as a tailor. Chana, Moishe, and their son, Shiele, have now received visas to Canada through him. They, too, will be leaving Germany soon.

" 'As long as there is life, there is hope.' Those words are my mother's legacy." I swallow hard.

"I wish Mala could stay in Boston. But her sponsor is the HIAS in New York. We would not dare ask for changes in destination. It may create complications. Still, she will be in America.

"How strange. Our destination was Boston and we arrived in New York. Mala is going to New York but is arriving in Boston. At least we will meet again, even if it is only for a few hours. We will be in a free country. Free to visit. Free to move from place to place. Maybe Chana and Yankl will be able to come to America one day." The words rush from my mouth.

Lillie's voice is soft and low. "Eddie and I, all of the cousins, wish we could take away the pain in your hearts. We are so happy that you have family to be reunited with."

She sighs. "We are the only family Morris has. He is the only survivor of the large family we had in Poland."

"Lillie, you are my family, too. Moniek and I are very lucky. We found family in America that truly cares about us. You are always here to help, to give your love and support."

I take her hand in mine. "Not all the survivors are that fortunate. I spoke to some whose families only came to see them once and brought a box of candy. That was the last they saw of them."

She gives my hand a warm squeeze. "That is sad. Very, very sad."

I caress her hand. "We appreciate the warmth and understanding you give us. You cannot heal our wounds. No one can. But having people who care helps."

10

"Moniek." I hold Moniek's hand in mine. "Remember how much we wanted our children to be born in America." Pictures of crowded displaced persons camps in Germany flash through my mind. "Remember the pain, the disappointment as the land of freedom stood closed to us after the gates of the death camps were finally opened by our liberators."

I take a deep breath. "Five years we waited. Our two sons were born in the displaced persons camps." I smile. "Our third child will be an American by birth. I am pregnant."

Moniek holds me tight. His face radiates a warm glow.

"Remember how we worried about having children, not knowing what the Nazis might have done to us in the concentration camps to prevent future Jewish generations. We survived. We have a family. Each child is a very special gift."

Tears glisten in his eyes.

"Will we manage the medical bills?" I whisper softly.

"We'll manage." His voice is strong and confident.

"I remember my mother telling a friend, 'Each child brings its own luck.' "

Moniek bites his lip. "I wish our children could know

the joy of having grandparents." He stares out the window.

I watch him silently. Our joy is woven with pain. "We cannot change the past, darling. But we can build a future." I hold his hand in mine. "Our children are the future."

He squeezes my hand gently.

We share our happy news with our neighbors, Berta and Jack. A cloud covers Berta's face. Her eyes well up with tears. I stare at her, bewildered. "Berta, are you all right? You look upset."

She bursts out crying. "Jack and I want a child so very, very much. We have everything to give to a child: a comfortable home, love, security. But we cannot have any children."

She grabs my hand suddenly, holds it in a tight grip. "Ruth, I beg of you." Her voice sounds strange, frightening. "Ruth, let us have your baby. We'll pay all the medical bills. We'll give you money to buy a comfortable home for your children. You would not have to live in this old house."

Her fingers dig into my flesh. "We will make life good for your children. Please. Give me your unborn child. Please. Please."

I pull my hand away from her. The wretchedness in her voice, the despair in her eyes, her horrifying request send chills down my spine. I move closer to Moniek.

"Berta. Are you out of your mind?" His eyes flash angrily. "You want us to sell our child? You must be crazy!"

"I may sound crazy. Maybe I am. My life is empty without a child."

Jack takes her hand. "Calm down, Berta, please, calm down," he whispers hoarsely.

"I cannot give you a child, Jack." She turns toward Moniek and me. "You are new in America. Life is not easy for newcomers. You have no money." She stops for a moment. "And you have two other children."

She stares wildly at us. "Jack and I can give your child so much."

The agony in her voice, the madness in her eyes, fill me with pity and horror. I swallow the lump in my throat. "Berta." My voice quivers. "Our children are not for sale!"

"Ruth, forgive her, please." Jack holds Berta tight as he pleads with me. "Please have pity on her. She is a good person." He lowers his voice. "You are not the first expectant mother she has done this to."

He wipes the tears from his face. "Have pity. Forgive her. She is a good person."

Berta buries her face in her hands and sobs bitterly. Jack leads her toward the door.

My heart cries for her.

11

October 30, 1950. Our third son is born in Brookline, Massachusetts, USA. An American citizen.

He is named after Moniek's mother, Chava. *Chava* is the feminine form of the Hebrew word for *life*. The masculine form is *Chaim*. We name our son Chaim in Hebrew, Harvey in English.

"Another name passed on," I whisper as I stare in wonder at the new miracle in my arms.

Moniek sits at the edge of the bed, his face radiant. "Each child brings its own luck. We have three healthy, beautiful sons."

He takes my hand in his. "You worried so about the bills. I have good news. The Jewish Family Service will help us with the bills."

Louie and Allen are overjoyed. A new brother, someone to play ball with. They touch his hands softly.

"I will need your help, boys." I smile. Louie is four years and two months old, Allen one year and three months old. They are pleased with whatever tasks I give them, bringing diapers or baby powder, or holding the baby bottle.

Lillie comes to help each day. I am grateful for her help, for her devotion.

My neighbors, Carl, Berta, and Jack, come to see the baby. They bring gifts. I feel sorry for Berta. Her eyes are moist. "Do you want to hold the baby, Berta?" I ask.

She nods. I take the baby from the cradle and put him into her arms. She holds him close to her. Her lips quiver. Jack looks at her, then turns toward me. "Thank you," he whispers. "Thank you."

12

Our family in Malden is warm and loving. Still, my heart yearns to be with my sister Mala in New York.

It was so wonderful to see her again when she, Yosef, and the children came to see us in Malden. We held each other tightly for a long time, our eyes overflowing with tears of joy. "We are in America. We are together again."

"I have to visit Mala in New York, Moniek. I must see her again." My voice trembles. "I will take the children; you have to work."

"How will you manage with three little ones on the train? Allen and Harvey are still in diapers, and Laibele— Louie"—he corrects himself—"is only a child."

"He may be a child, but he is a great help to me," I assure him, smiling. "We will manage."

A shadow covers Moniek's face. "I understand your wanting to see your sister. Not too many of us are that lucky. But. . . ."

He stares at the window silently. I take his hand in mine. "I know. Each time we say good-bye, the fear that we will not see each other again returns."

He turns his face toward me, presses my hand silently.

"The scars of the past will always be with us. Each time we said good-bye, it was forever. I, too, live with the fear of saying good-bye." I move close to him. "We will be gone only a short time."

Moniek looks so forlorn as he puts us on the train. I feel guilty for leaving him alone.

"We will be home soon, Daddy," Louie calls happily.

"Bye-bye, Daddy." Allen waves his little hand.

"Have a safe trip." Moniek's voice cracks. "Have a safe trip."

The train begins to move slowly, then faster and faster. Tears choke me as I watch Moniek disappearing from my side.

Bubbling with excitement, Louie places himself by the window. I make Allen and Harvey comfortable on the seat.

"You have a lot of courage, young lady." A woman smiles pleasantly at me. "Traveling alone from Boston to New York with three little ones, two in diapers yet."

She watches me as I change the wet diapers.

"You look like a child yourself. It must be hard on you. I do not think I would have the strength."

I glance at her quickly. She is young, healthy looking, well dressed. What does she know about strength? *You look like a child yourself.* Was I ever a child?

"It is so much work, so much trouble to raise a family," she proclaims loudly.

I turn toward her angrily. "Children are a blessing, not trouble. I am very, very lucky to have children." Screaming mothers, reaching toward children being torn from their arms by the Nazis, flash before me.

The tone of my voice startles her. "I am sorry. I did not mean to upset you." Her voice is subdued, bewildered.

"I am sorry for my angry outburst," I murmur softly. "Children are the greatest treasure." I take my baby, Harvey, into my lap. Louie and Allen sit at my sides. I feel at peace again.

Mala and Yosef wait at the train station. They rush toward us. I suddenly remember Mala rushing toward me at the displaced persons camp in Leipheim, Germany, after seven years of separation, of anguish, of hope. I also remember the pain of saying good-bye.

Now we are here, in America. Together again. We hold each other tight. No need for words.

13

My neighbor Carl smiles broadly. "Ruth, I must tell you how impressed I am with the way you've learned English in the two years you've lived in America."

"Thank you, Carl. It is very important to me that I learn to speak, read, and write English. America is my home now."

"How many other languages do you speak, Ruth?"

"Well, I speak Yiddish, Polish, German." My voice shakes. "I do not like to speak German. It only brings back the ugly names the Nazis called us. It brings back the suffering again."

Carl sits near me on the front steps. "It must have been hard to be a slave." He stares at the peaceful scenery, the trees covered with green leaves, the quiet street. "I can't think of you as a slave. Doing hard labor. Alone. Guarded. Beaten."

His voice fills with anger. "Why is there so much hatred? So much prejudice?"

Louie tosses his ball toward Carl. Carl catches it quickly, tosses it back. "Children aren't born prejudiced. People are *taught* to hate because one looks different. Because one speaks differently. Because one worships differently. I know about prejudice. I know about slavery. My ancestors were slaves."

I watch some people strolling slowly up the street. "I wonder if they know the value of freedom, Carl?"

"I'm sure they take freedom for granted. Not to mention the right to choose their leaders." Carl raises his voice. "I wonder how many will vote in the upcoming elections, Ruth."

"I wish I could vote, Carl. But I have to wait three more years, until I am an American citizen, to have that privilege."

We sit silently for a while, each absorbed in thoughts of our own.

"I like what the candidate for senator, John F. Kennedy, stands for. I think he knows the value of freedom. There must be something I can do to help him get elected."

"I think he'll make a good senator. He seems like a good man, Ruth."

"I must find a way to do something worthwhile, even if I cannot vote, Carl. I must."

I contact Moniek's cousin Phil, who puts me in touch with the Kennedy campaign. I am given literature to distribute on a Malden street. With my three little boys helping me, I hand out fliers.

"Please vote for John F. Kennedy," Laibele adds each time he hands someone a flier. "Please vote."

People stare at the strange sight: a woman speaking with a foreign accent, with three little children by her side, eagerly passing out fliers, urging the passersby to vote.

Some stop to talk to us. "Why should I vote for Kennedy?" an elderly man asks, challenging. "All politicians are the same to me. I don't trust any of them. Why should I take the trouble to vote at all?"

"I feel that Kennedy cares about the people." My voice betrays my nervousness. "But please vote for anyone you feel is a better candidate, as long as you use your right to vote."

"The right to vote. It's no big deal," he replies with a sarcastic smile on his lips. "It's no big deal."

"You are taking your freedom to choose too much for granted." The anger in my voice startles him. "You are free to choose your government. You are free to choose your leaders. Do not give up that freedom."

Others stop, listen.

"I know the pain of slavery. I know the value of freedom. Please, listen! You are free to make a difference! Do not give up that privilege." I feel drained. "I cannot vote yet. I am not yet an American citizen. But you can. Please vote."

"Please vote." Louie hands out fliers again. "Please vote."

I search the faces of the onlookers as they take the fliers

from my child's little hands. Did I reach them? Did I make a difference? I hope so. I hope so.

"John F. Kennedy was elected senator, Louie." I share the great news with my son.

"We did well, Mommy. Right?" A smile covers his face.

"We did well, my son. We did well." I take him in my arms. "We did well."

14

I watch my children at play. Their voices ring gaily in the air. It feels good to see them happy, carefree.

I marvel at my son, Louie. He came from a different world, spoke only Yiddish. How naturally English flows from his lips now. He plays cowboys and Indians, chases after a baseball. Games learned from his new playmates.

"May I go across the street to Chris's house and take Allen with me, Mommy?" he calls cheerfully after a short conference with his friend.

"Who is there to keep an eye on you boys?"

"My grandmother will watch us, Mrs. Sender," Chris shouts. "My grandmother will take care of us."

"Okay, Louie, but hold Allen's hand as you cross the street."

"I will, I will," Louie calls as he takes Allen by the hand. Allen's big, blue eyes glow with excitement. He loves to go with his brother to visit friends. He likes to be treated like the older kids, even though he is only three years old and Louie is six.

I play with Harvey, who is still a toddler. His brown eyes twinkle merrily. I feel happy. I feel at peace.

The children return near dinnertime. Allen carries a small paper bag in his hands. "Chris's grandmother bakes good cookies," he proclaims. "She sent some for Harvey. I wish I had a grandmother to bake cookies for us."

Louie listens silently to Allen's happy chatter. Suddenly he asks, "Mommy, why don't we have a grandmother? A grandfather? Chris has two grandmothers and two grandfathers. But we don't have any."

Voices of Holocaust survivors, voices filled with agony, ring in my ears. *Someday your children will ask why they have no grandparents, aunts, uncles. How will you answer?*

My heart beats fast. How do I answer? How do I answer?

"Why don't we have any grandparents?" Louie asks again. His eyes are glued to my face.

"They died." I bite my lips.

"Did they die because they were very, very old?"

I sit down. My child waits for an answer. "They were not old."

"So why did they die?"

"They were killed." My voice is a painful whisper.

"Who killed them?" His eyes flash angrily.

"The Nazis."

"Why? Why did they kill my grandparents?" he shouts.

I take him on my lap. Hold him tight. Tears choke me. "Because they were Jews."

He stares at me, bewildered.

"The Nazis were evil. They killed many, many Jews."

"But the Jews did not do anything to them."

"No. The Jews did not do anything to them."

"So why didn't other people stop the Nazis from killing the Jews?"

My head spins. How do I tell a six-year-old child about hatred, prejudice, indifference? "I, too, ask why."

"Don't cry, Mommy." He touches my face softly. "I love you, Mommy."

15

One day Moniek returns from work carrying a big package. "Louie! Allen! Harvey!"

His voice rings with excitement as he gathers his three sons around him. "I have something special for you."

"What is it, Daddy? A present?"

Moniek holds the package tightly. He is grinning broadly.

"Let's see it. Let's see it," they plead.

"Well, let's see it, Moniek." I, too, become curious. "Stop teasing the kids. Let's see it."

Slowly, carefully, he opens the paper bag. The kids' eyes follow his every move as three neatly wrapped packages appear before us. "This one is for Louie. This one for Allen. This one for Harvey."

Moniek's eyes glow with pleasure. "Louie, you open yours first."

Louie rips the paper quickly. "A cowboy suit! A cowboy hat! A holster and gun! A real cowboy suit!"

Allen and Harvey stare in awe at the black cowboy suit, the hat, the holster, the gun. The dream of each little boy.

Eagerly they, too, rip the paper with trembling hands. "I have a cowboy suit, too," Allen shouts, overjoyed. "A cowboy hat!"

"Me, too! Me, too!" Harvey jumps up and down.

"Let's try them on." Louie quickly changes. Allen and Harvey follow his example, laughing, shouting happily.

Within minutes three little cowboys stand before us, grinning proudly.

Moniek's eyes glow, but the sight of the gun in Louie's holster makes me shiver. Each time I see the kids in the street pull their toy guns, shouting, "Bang! Bang! You're dead!" I shrivel inside. "Moniek, I do not want our children to have guns."

"They're only toys, Ruth. A cowboy has to have a gun. I did not buy any for the little ones."

"It's only make-believe. I won't shoot anybody for real, Mommy. May I keep the gun, please?"

All eyes are on me. If I say no, I will spoil a very special day for them. I feel torn.

"It's only make-believe, Mommy. All the big boys have guns in their holsters. Please, Mommy, please," Louie insists.

"All the other big boys have toy guns," Moniek echoes. "Toy guns do not kill."

I feel defeated. "Please, do not bring home any more guns, even if they are only toys, Moniek." I turn to Louie. "Because Daddy already got you the toy gun, you may keep it."

"Hurray! Thank you, Daddy!" the three of them shout as they run quickly to show off to the other kids.

"I had to buy them those suits. Even if they cost a lot." Moniek turns to me. "I want my sons to have the same things other children have."

I see the determined look in his eyes. I know how he feels. We were deprived of our childhoods. Our children should know the joys of childhood.

"Where did you get the money for the suits, Moniek?" I ask suddenly. "You said they were expensive."

"Promise you will not be angry, darling." He takes my hand in his. "I got paid today." He searches for words. "Well . . . I used this week's pay. . . ."

I stare at him. "The whole week's pay? We cannot afford that."

"We will manage. The joy on the children's faces, in their voices. . . ." He watches the kids through the window. "We will manage. We will manage."

16

"I wish we could be together again," I read in the letter from my sister Chana in Canada. Tears glide over my face. If only we could be together again, Mala, Chana, Yankl, and I. We lost one another. Found one another . . . only to be separated again. Chana and my brother Yankl are in Canada. But Mala and I live in America. We are kept apart by borders. I put my head down and cry bitterly.

"What is wrong, Ruth?" Moniek stares at me, frightened by my red, swollen eyes. "Every time I come home, you look like you cried all day." He sighs heavily. "We manage okay. Our family is kind and warm. The kids are happy. So why are you crying?"

"I miss my sisters, my brother." My eyes well up with tears. "Let's move to New York, Moniek, please."

He looks startled. "I have a job here, we have an apartment, Louie is in school. We have family here who brought us to America. We cannot just pick ourselves up and leave."

Pictures of men, women, and children carrying their belongings on their backs, marching to unknown destinations, appear before my eyes. "Moniek. We picked ourselves up each time we were ordered to leave one place for another. We had no choice. Moving for us is not hard anymore.

"But now we have a choice. We are free to choose where we want to live. You will find work. You are a hard worker. We will stay with Mala and Yosef until we find an apartment. School for Louie is no problem. He is a good student, and kids make new friends. Our family here will understand." The words stream from my mouth.

"I want to be with my sister. Please, let's move to New York."

"But we are settled here, Ruth."

"I have to be with my sister. You understand that."

"Yes, I understand that." His voice quivers. "I understand that."

We sit silently for a long time. Painful, worrisome thoughts race through my mind. What if he does not find work? What if Mala has no room for us? She has only a two-bedroom apartment; they are four. Where will she put five more people? Am I being unreasonable, selfish?

I feel Moniek's eyes on me. I am sure he, too, struggles with many unanswered questions. "I cannot watch you cry. You want to leave? Okay, write to Mala and Yosef. Let's hear what they have to say."

I throw my arms around him, hold him tight.

"I want you to be happy. We suffered enough." His voice is low. "We suffered enough."

I write to Mala. Her reply is a mixture of joy and concern.

"You worry about our having room for you," she writes.

> Remember, my dear little sister, we were nine people in Lodz, Grandma, Mama, and seven children. We lived in two rooms. We managed just fine. So we are nine again. And now we have four rooms. We will be happy to share whatever we have with you so that we can be together again.
>
> Finding a job for Moniek may be more of a problem. Still, we must hope that everything will work out well. I do not have to tell you: As long as there is life, there is hope.

"As long as there is life, there is hope," I whisper. "As long as there is life, there is hope." Many times when all looked dark and hopeless, I remembered Mama's words. They helped me hold on to life. Hope. Hope. Hope.

17

November 1952. Mala and I are finally reunited. My sons are with their cousins Abramek and Esther again. Abramek, twelve years old now, tall and skinny, quickly takes charge of the younger children.

The displaced persons camp in Leipheim, Germany, is vivid in my mind. Abramek, six, sees Laibele, five months old, for the first time. The joy of having a cousin radiates from Abramek's pale face. He gazes with awe at the tiny member of his family. "I am your cousin, Abramek. I'll take good care of you, Laibele. I am a big boy."

Now Laibele is six years and four months old. Abramek is still the big boy. My heart sings. How wonderful to see them together again.

Mala and Yosef's home is filled with warmth. Yosef works in a tailor shop. "I am very, very happy. I have a job. I support my family. We have a roof over our heads. America is a golden land," he proclaims. He entertains us with anecdotes from the Yiddish theater, always close to his heart.

"Yosef, you love the Yiddish theater. You are a talented actor and director. In the displaced persons camps, you traveled from camp to camp to bring Yiddish theater to the remnants of our people. Why don't you find work on the Yiddish stage?" I ask softly.

He lowers his eyes. "In the camps, the Yiddish theater was needed to help us rise from the ashes and live again. We were homeless. We lived on charity. Now we have a home. We do not want any charity, Rifkele. I love the theater . . . but you cannot support your family by being a Yiddish actor." His face brightens. "My family comes first."

"Yosef, you have a captive audience right here."

He smiles softly. "You are a good audience, a very welcome audience."

One evening, he sings an old Yiddish folk song in a nostalgic voice.

"My childhood years,
I lost you.
Forever you remain in my memory."

His eyes rest sadly on my face. "I am older than you. I had a childhood. But, you, you were only thirteen when the Nazi beast trampled our lives." He sighs heavily. "You were robbed of your childhood."

Mala's eyes well up with tears. She nods her head sadly. "You had no childhood, Riva."

Her eyes have a faraway look. "We were all robbed of

our childhoods. I was only eleven when Daddy died suddenly during a typhoid epidemic." She wipes the corners of her eyes. "Mama was a young widow with six children and expecting the seventh. The baby born shortly after Daddy's death was named after Daddy and Grandpa, Avrom Moishe."

We wait silently for her to compose herself.

"I had to help Mama support seven children." Her voice is very low. "Because I started the Jewish day school, the Borchov Shul, at six, I graduated at twelve. I took evening classes to further my education and went to work full-time in a weaving plant."

Abramek stares at her, wide-eyed. "Mommy. You were the same age as I am now. Did they let you work in a factory at twelve?"

She touches Abramek's face softly. "I had to be fourteen to get working papers for a part-time job, delivering newspapers. I looked older than twelve. We had a cousin, Esther Minska. She was nineteen. I used her birth certificate. My maiden name was the same as hers, Minska."

Her eyes well up with tears again. "Esther, too, died during the Holocaust.

"I still see Mama's tear-stricken face as she watched me disappear into the grayish light of dawn. I still hear her voice. 'My poor child, you lost your childhood.' "

I wipe the tears gliding over my cheeks. Mala silently

squeezes my hand. "Chana and Yankl, too, had to start working at an early age."

My voice cracks. "I was robbed of my childhood by the Nazis. You were robbed of your childhood by poverty."

"But we had happy times. We had family, friends."

Yosef gazes from one of us to the other, a soft smile playing on his lips. "Remember the love. The warmth of your mother's touch. The songs. The smiles. No one can rob us of our memories."

18

I have wonderful news. My friends Karola and Tola are in New York. Our long, pain-filled journey from slavery to freedom finally brought us all here. We shared the agony of the death camps, the joy of liberation, the desperate search for a place to call home. We are here. A home at last.

Is this all real? Is the present only a dream? Was the past only a nightmare?

I hear my children's laughter. The present is real. I look at Moniek. The blue numbers tattooed on his arm in Auschwitz scream silently. The past is real.

You must forget the past.

You must live for the future.

It is too painful to speak about it.

It is too painful to hear about it.

Voices. Voices. Voices. Angry voices. Tired voices. Annoyed voices. They race through my mind, try to drown each other out.

Our scars are too deep.

We had mothers, fathers, brothers, sisters. They were murdered by the Nazis. Should we also wipe away the memory of them?

I feel anger rising within me. If we wipe away the memory of them, they will be murdered all over again.

I think of Tola. She lost her husband and children, murdered by the Nazis. She survived. Remarried. Has a son. A new life. But how can she forget the past? Can she sing a lullaby to her child without remembering singing the same lullaby to her children who were murdered? How can she forget?

Can I hear a mother and daughter speaking softly to one another without remembering my mother's soft voice, her smile, her touch? No. We cannot forget. We must not forget.

If your heart is heavy, cry when no one sees you. When you are with people, smile. Mama's voice.

19

Apartments are very hard to find. Each apartment is rented before it is even vacant. To demand money for vacating an apartment is illegal, but under the pretext of selling furniture to the new tenants, the current ones ask for large sums of money.

The superintendents of the buildings also demand bribes. In most cases the superintendents are in charge of renting. It is frustrating and unfair. Still, this is the only way to find housing with reasonable rent.

My friends Karola and Oscar live with their son, Maxie, on Garden Street in the Bronx. It is a quiet, residential street across from the Bronx Zoo. "I have to find you an apartment here." Karola's voice rings with determination. "We were neighbors and friends in the ghetto of Lodz. We stayed together in the death camps, in the labor camps, on the wooden planks that were our home."

She takes a deep breath. "After liberation Oscar and I shared a home with you and Moniek in Wroclaw. Now I have to see to it that we remain neighbors." Her eyes flash. "I'll do it. You'll see."

Karola makes daily rounds to the superintendents of the neighborhood buildings. "Do you know of any upcoming vacancy?" She asks mothers waiting for their children at the front of the school. "Do you know of any upcoming vacancy?" She stops people in the street. "Do you know of any upcoming vacancy?"

Her efforts pay off. "775 Garden Street will soon have a vacancy," someone informs her. She speaks to the superintendent.

"There is a three-bedroom apartment coming up."

He asks a fee for showing the apartment. The present tenants insist on selling us their old furniture.

With Mala and Yosef's help, we raise the money. Five hundred dollars for "the furniture," fifty dollars for the superintendent.

In January 1953, we move into an apartment at 775 Garden Street, the Bronx, New York. In the Land of the Free, Karola and I are neighbors again. We were children when we first met. We faced death. We survived. Now our sons attend together Public School 32 in the Bronx, in the United States of America.

My eyes well up with tears of joy as I watch our children study. Our children. The Jewish children that were not to be born had Hitler succeeded in his master plan to annihilate the Jews.

Grafenort, Germany. Karola and I dig ditches for the Germans to hide in from the bombs. Karola smiles sadly. "It is May 3, Riva. Your birthday."

"This is your last birthday, Jew." The Nazi guard's

sarcastic voice rings in my ears. "By next year you will all be dead."

But we held on to life. Our children, born in displaced persons camps in Germany, study American history together. I listen to their excited voices. My heart sings.

Together Karola and I shop at the grocery store. The shelves, full of so many different foods, make our hearts beat faster. We stare silently at each other. How many years did we dream of a piece of bread?

Is this real? I have family. I have friends. Is it real?

20

Moniek's sullen face, his frustration at not finding a well-paying job, makes me feel guilty. In Boston he had a good job. In New York he goes from one job to another. In Boston he was a member of the meat-packers' union, but the union in New York does not seem to be able to find work for him. He is angry, bitter.

"We will manage, Moniek." I take his hand in mine.

"Manage . . . with what?" His voice is a painful whisper.

"We are surviving."

"I was hoping to make life better for you." He stares at the window.

"Life is better, Moniek." I hold his hand tightly. "I am with my sister."

His eyes remain fixed on the window. "I had a good job. Now I feel lost. I wish I could jump off a bridge."

I swallow hard. "Don't give up hope. You'll find a better job."

His agony-filled eyes, his sullen face fill me with terror, fill me with anger. "You survived five years of Auschwitz. You did not give up. Look at us. We are alive. We have a family."

He lowers his head. "I feel helpless."

"How will you help us by jumping off a bridge?" I wipe the tears from my face.

His eyes are still fixed on the window. "If hope is lost, all is lost," I whisper softly.

He squeezes my hand silently.

21

I have gallstone attacks often. The pain is becoming harder and harder to endure. I remember the first time I had an attack. I was a child, in the ghetto of Lodz, Poland.

I feel Mama's arms holding me tight. "It will pass. It will pass. My poor child." Her trembling voice betrays her agony, her helplessness.

Without the aid of X rays, by the symptoms only, the doctor determines that I have gallstones. "I never heard of a young child having gallstones."

"But, Mrs. Minska"—he looks at my mother sadly— "here everything is possible."

"What can you do to help my child, Doctor?" Mama's voice quivers. "She is in so much pain."

He stares at me, frustration written all over his face. "A child with an adult disease. I have never seen a child with gallstones." He lowers his head. "If the pain of hunger is not enough, now this. . . ."

He looks up at me. "The only thing I can do now is give you valerian drops to ease the pain." Then he turns to Mama. "If you have a little sugar, give some to Riva to take away the bitter taste of the medicine."

Mama stares at the doctor. "Valerian drops, Doctor? They are used to revive one who has fainted?"

"We use what we have. The drops will help Riva catch her breath when she has an attack." He sighs. "Soon the medicine supply we still have will end. And then what?"

Mama's eyes well up with tears. She wipes them quickly.

"Should I apply heat when she gets an attack? Will it help, Doctor?"

"It may make her feel more comfortable, Mrs. Minska. Surgery is the only solution."

Mama's face turns white. She looks as if she is about to faint.

"No need to get upset, Mrs. Minska. Even if you agreed to the surgery, we cannot operate here. In the ghetto doctors are helpless."

The word *surgery* frightens me. I remember the panic that overtook families when someone had to have surgery. The fear of going to a hospital. The fear of death hanging heavily in the air. The tears. The prayers. The gloom.

For once I am grateful that I am in the ghetto. Here they cannot perform surgery on me.

That was 1940. Now it is 1954. The fear of surgery is still with me. I remember the displaced persons camps in Germany. Each time I had a gallstone attack and surgery was suggested, I panicked. The thought of having to enter a hospital in Germany, with German doctors performing surgery on me, filled me with horror.

I saw myself over and over again in Germany, 1944. My concentration camp number, 55082, and the yellow Star of David visible on my old, oversized coat. Escorted by a Nazi guard, in search of medical help for blood poisoning, marching in the gutters of the beautiful town of Glatz. Again and again, I heard the German doctors chasing me from the hospitals. *We do not treat Jews! We do not treat Jews!*

In the displaced persons camp I told myself that I must hold on until we were out of Germany. I am in America now. The attacks are very severe and frequent. I know that surgery cannot be postponed much longer. I look at my three children, and fear grips my heart. What if I do not survive the surgery?

The doctor sees the fear in my eyes. "I understand how you feel. It is major surgery. Any surgery is serious. But most people survive. You will be okay. Your children will have a healthy mother, not one who doubles up in pain each time she has an attack." He takes me by the hand. "Remember, this is 1954. Medicine has made a lot of progress. You will be okay."

"Doctor"—my face feels hot—"I have to wait a little longer."

He looks puzzled. "What is wrong with next week? The longer you wait, the worse it gets."

"I have to see my sisters and my brother before I go to the hospital."

"So? Go see them tomorrow." He sounds annoyed.

"I can see my sister Mala. She lives in the Bronx. But I need time to see my sister Chana and my brother, Yankl. They live in Montreal, Canada."

"I know where Montreal is." His eyes move slowly over my face.

"I have to see them once more."

"You're afraid that you will never see them again. You

must not think that way." He raises his voice, then quickly lowers it again. "I'm sorry. Maybe I'm being insensitive. One who did not live through your agonies, your painful separations, could never really understand. Go see your family. I'll see you after you return from Canada."

22

It is the first time that I am leaving the borders of the United States. I feel very nervous. Moniek remains at home. He has to work. I am with three small children on a train that is taking us out of the land we waited so long to enter. A horrible thought crosses my mind. What if they refuse to let us back in?

Louie, Allen, and I have Alien Registration cards, called green cards. This means we are still here on a temporary basis, waiting to become American citizens. Harvey, my youngest son, is the only one who is a citizen. He was born in the United States of America.

I feel overwhelming panic as I look at my children. What if. . . . Cold sweat drips down my forehead. I wipe my face quickly. I must not scare the children. But what if. . . . The terrible thought keeps nagging at me.

I stare out the window. The passing landscape is green, open, inviting. It speaks to me of freedom.

Again I check our green cards, Harvey's birth certificate. It is all here. Proof that we have the right to return.

I look at the people around me. Can they see the fear in my eyes? A woman sitting across from us reads a book. Would she understand my fear? I wonder what it feels like not to be afraid.

My heart pounds as we get closer to the Canadian border. I hold our documents tightly in my hand, waiting for questions, checkpoints.

"We're in Canada now," the woman across from me announces calmly. She seems amused by my bewildered look. "This must be your first time on a train to Canada."

I nod.

"It's very simple." She chuckles. "Sometimes they ask for your papers." She returns to reading her book.

It is very simple echoes in my ears.

At the station in Montreal, they are waiting. My sister Chana. My brother Yankl. Their families. I hold them in my arms again and silently count the years of separation. I was thirteen the first time we were torn apart. We lost one another for seven years. We found one another in the displaced persons camps in Germany, only to be torn apart again. It is six years since I last saw Yankl and four years since I last saw Chana.

I am a mother of three now, Chana a mother of two,
Yankl a father of three.

I hear the happy voices of our children. My tears roll
quietly over my face. If we could all be together. . . .

23

"How do you feel, Ruth?" the doctor asks softly as he
enters my hospital room. "We took out your gallbladder.
You had many large stones. Fourteen years." He sighs.
"Half of your life you lived in pain."

He presses my abdomen lightly. I moan. "I'm sorry. It
will get better, you'll see." He squeezes my hand warmly.
"You will be okay."

For a while I am still in pain and wonder if the surgery
helped. But slowly the attacks stop. I *am* okay.

24

My three sons are all in school already. They grow
quickly. They were just babies, and now they are all in
school. I cried when Harvey, too, disappeared into the
school building. I felt all alone.

Slowly pass days, years fly by fast. I remember a poem from my childhood.

I join the Parent-Teacher Association, become a class mother. I help with the children going on a school trip and with holiday activities. I love being part of school life.

Many times I think of the children in my kindergarten class in the displaced persons camp in Germany. I remember their bewildered eyes. Their frightened whispers.

Why do we live here?

Did the war not end yet?

Will they come back again, the bad people?

Is it all right to sing?

I watch the happy children rushing through the bright school building and wonder how the children I worked with are doing now. Did they adjust? Do they feel safe?

I, too, have a lot to learn in the land of freedom. I enroll in English classes for adults.

The students are of different ages and from many countries. I listen to the sounds of their accents, trying to determine what parts of the world they come from. I wonder about their pasts, their lives here. Each student seems so eager to learn, but as soon as class is over, they quickly disappear into the world outside school. Everyone is always rushing, rushing, rushing.

My eyes linger with admiration on the round, smiling

face of Mrs. Shaw, our teacher. Clearly, slowly, she pronounces new English words. Her brown eyes twinkle as she listens to her students' efforts to learn the new vocabulary. A big grin covers her face each time one of us does well.

"She is a wonderful teacher. She loves teaching," I whisper to an elderly woman at the next desk at the end of the session.

The woman nods. "I have been coming here for years."

"For years?"

The woman's pale blue eyes have a faraway look. Her voice is very low. "I came to America as a young girl from Russia, to escape the czar, the pogroms, the poverty." She sighs. "I worked in sweatshops. I had no time for school. I married young, had four children. I had to help support my family. I had no time for school."

Her face lights up. "We worked hard to give our children a good education. My children are all professionals." She stops for a moment, as if reflecting, and sighs. "Now I have too much time. My husband passed away five years ago." Tears glisten in her eyes. "I miss him." She wipes her eyes quickly with a handkerchief. "The children are grown. Busy with their own lives. Now I have time for school. So I keep coming back." She smiles sadly. "That's my story."

"Each one here has a story," I murmur.

I hear voices in my head. *You have a story to tell.*

You survived.

We perished.

Remember us.

Remember us.

"So when did you come here, child?" The soft voice of my elderly classmate mingles with the voices of those who perished. "When did you come to America?" she asks again.

"Five years ago." My voice is low.

"Where are you from?"

"Poland."

She stares at me as if seeing me for the first time. "You are a Holocaust survivor?" Her eyes fill with horror.

I nod my head silently.

Her eyes glued to my face, she whispers, "You are so warm. So nice." Her voice cracks. "I did not know."

I shrug my shoulders. Bite my lips.

We should be running around mad. Voices of survivors ring in my ears.

We should be running around mad.

She takes my hand, holds it tight. I feel the trembling of her fingers. "I did not know. You are so nice. I did not know." She turns, leaves the classroom without looking at me.

You have a story to tell.

I did not know.

Voices of the past and present mingle as I ride the bus

home. There I throw my coat on the bed. Take paper and pen in hand. I stare at the blank paper before me.

You survived. You survived. Voices murmur in my ear.

Suddenly today disappears. In the barbed-wire ghetto cage, the Nazi guards surround me, hold me in their steel grip.

It is September 1942. Lodz, Poland. I hear Mama's pain-filled screams as she is torn away from her children. I see her horror-filled eyes, her arms stretching toward us. I see the ghetto policeman pulling her back into the wagon. Taking her away from us.

I feel the darkness, the emptiness, as the four of us are left alone. I am sixteen. Motele fifteen. Laibele thirteen. Moishele eleven. I feel their presence.

Remember. Remember.

My pen moves swiftly over the paper. I remember. Tears blind me. I keep on writing. I remember.

I gaze at the writing before me, and the pages written in the ghetto, recording our daily struggle for life, flash before my eyes. I carried them with me to the gates of hell, Auschwitz. They vanished, just as the people in my life vanished.

I feel worn out and slump heavily into a chair. My eyes fall on a magazine on the kitchen table. *Reader's Digest.* I like its "First Person" stories. What if I take a chance? This is a first-person story. . . .

I am excited. I need a title. My mind wanders back to the ghetto cage. I shiver. That is it. That is the title of my story. "The Cage."

I tremble as I write. "The Cage. By Ruth Minsky Sender." I fold the paper, address the envelope, run to the mailbox across the street, toss the letter in quickly. I feel a tremendous sense of relief.

I wait impatiently for an answer from *Reader's Digest*. Finally it comes. They are sorry. They have no room for my story in their magazine.

I feel let down. I put the story in the drawer, remembering stories I put in the drawer in the ghetto of Lodz. Stories that were never read. "I will not give up," I proclaim as I straighten my back, defiant. "I will try again."

25

My sister Mala teaches a Jewish kindergarten. I watch her slowly, patiently teach the little ones a Yiddish song. The glow on her face reflects her joy in teaching a new Jewish generation.

The kindergarten, formed and supported mostly by

Holocaust survivors, carries the name of Michael Klepfish, a Jewish martyr who gave his life fighting the Nazis during the uprising of the Warsaw ghetto in Poland. On a wall in the center of the room hangs his picture. You are the future, dear children. You must not forget the past, his gentle eyes speak as they watch over the happy, playful children.

The sound of children singing a Yiddish song brings back the muffled voices of children in the ghetto, secretly studying, softly singing songs of hope, reciting poems about a better tomorrow. I see them before me. Bony skeletons holding on to life in forbidden study groups with a song, a poem, a story of a world that once had family, freedom, food.

"With a little saw,
Saw, saw, saw,
With a little hammer,
Clap, clap, clap,
With a little plane,
Plane, plane, plane,
Children build themselves a home."

The voices of Mala's kindergarten class carry me again from the past to the present. The sorrow of the past mingles with the joy of today. The children form a circle, clap their hands joyfully. Their voices ring like little bells.

"Saw, saw, saw,
Clap, clap, clap,

Plane, plane, plane,
Children build themselves a home."

My heart beats fast as I clap my hands to the beat of their song. "We, too, are building a new home. We are building a new tomorrow from the ashes of yesterday. We who survived," I whisper.

I feel Mala's gaze on me. Our eyes meet. Tears glide over her cheeks. She takes my hand and pulls me gently into the circle of singing and dancing children.

"Clap hands,
Clap, clap, clap,
Stomp feet,
Stomp, stomp, stomp.
Hands are clapping,
Feet are stomping.
Only work
Can make life sweet."

I clap my hands. Stomp my feet. Sing. "Only work can make life sweet."

Arbeit macht frei. "Work makes you free."

The towering sign at the gates of Auschwitz, the gates of hell, suddenly is before me again: *Arbeit macht frei.*

I stomp my feet defiantly, surrounded by singing and dancing Jewish children, in a kindergarten organized by Holocaust survivors.

26

Mala and I wait nervously at a pier in New York harbor. Soon we will meet, for the first time, our cousin Jose Strauss, from Argentina.

I watch the small vessels coming and going and remember my journey on the *General Greely,* a huge transport ship, five years ago, from a displaced persons camp in Germany to the land of freedom, America. After all the pain and wandering, a home at last, a place where I belong.

Now I, the new immigrant, wait to welcome to America a cousin I have never met, the son of my father's sister, Aunt Emma. He was born in Argentina, a land I know only from letters Aunt Emma wrote when I was a child in Poland. His mother left Poland as a young woman. My parents remained. We are only a few years apart in age.

How very, very different our lives turned out. He lived his childhood and his teens surrounded by family, comfort, and peace, striving to become a doctor. He reached his goal and is coming to America to specialize. His loving family bid him good-bye and wished him luck. I, too, had goals. I hoped to become a teacher. I hoped to become a writer. My unfulfilled dreams still linger.

I look at Mala. Her face is covered by a cloud. Is she thinking the same thoughts? "Soon he will be here, our cousin from Argentina," I say softly.

Then a frightening thought enters my mind. What if we meet our cousin and are separated by a language barrier? "Mala, how will we communicate with our cousin? We do not speak Spanish. You think he may speak Yiddish? Aunt Emma writes to us in Yiddish."

Mala sighs. "I hope he speaks English."

"I hope we know him when he arrives, Mala. We do not know what he looks like. We only know that he is traveling as ship's doctor."

A new vessel appears in the distance. I watch it come closer. "Do you think he is on this boat? It's so strange to meet a member of the family and not know him."

"It is strange." Mala, too, stares at the arriving boat. "We came to America to meet a cousin from Argentina."

We watch a group of people disembark from the newly docked vessel. Mala quickly checks the name against the name in the letter from Aunt Emma. "This is it!" she shouts.

We move quickly forward. The new arrivals look worn out from the long journey.

We approach one man. "Do you know Dr. Jose Strauss?"

He stares at us. "No English. No English."

We ask another. "Do you know Dr. Jose Strauss?"

He mumbles something we do not understand. Mala and I look at each other, frustrated.

"I know Dr. Strauss." A man, speaking English, approaches. "We are friends from Argentina." He points to another man next to him. "We came here to meet him. We, too, are doctors who came to specialize in America.

"Jose will be out soon." His eyes move from us to the vessel. "We were told that there was a medical emergency during the journey. Jose is waiting for the patient to be taken to the hospital."

"Could you point him out? He is a cousin we have never met," Mala says.

"I see." He smiles politely.

A man of medium build, in his twenties, with dark, curly hair, leaves the vessel, his eyes searching the faces of the people on the dock. A big grin lights up his face as he waves to the men next to us, calling to them in Spanish.

"That is your cousin, Dr. Jose Strauss." They smile.

"He looks Spanish," I whisper to Mala. "He does not look like a relative."

"He was born in Argentina. We were born in Poland. The land of one's birth may make a difference," she replies as the men greet one another warmly.

"Ladies, this is your cousin Jose Strauss from Argentina." One of them bows politely as he does the introduction. "Jose, these ladies are your American cousins."

American cousins. I like the sound of those words.

We smile at one another awkwardly for a moment. Then, as if we had known one another all our lives, we embrace warmly.

"My family sends its love," Jose says softly.

"He speaks English, Mala. He speaks English." I smile happily. "We were worried about the language barrier. I am so happy we can communicate, Jose."

"Slow down, please. You speak too fast for me, Ruth."

"Sorry. I forgot what it is like to follow a new language. Does it sound as if I have hot potatoes in my mouth and have to keep my mouth from getting burned?"

"Yes, it does. Yes, it does." He laughs.

We all join in.

27

May 16, 1955. Moniek and I stand surrounded by tense, nervous applicants for United States citizenship. We are gathered at the Southern District Court of New York, waiting with hearts pounding for the magic moment when we will be proclaimed citizens of the United States of America, the moment we have waited for, for so very, very long.

I hear a judge speak of the duty, obligations, and responsibilities of citizenship, the freedoms guaranteed under the Constitution of the United States of America. My head spins. Five years of studying English, American government, American history. Long hours of homework while the children slept. Tests leading to my goal: American citizenship. I made it.

The stern face of a government official flashes before me. I am back in his office. "Why do you want to be an American citizen?"

"Because I will not feel free until I am a citizen. Until I know where I belong." The words come from my heart. But what if he does not believe me? Can he send us back? I wonder if he can see the fear in my eyes, hear the pounding of my heart.

"You are a Polish citizen. Why did you leave Poland?"

I sit at the edge of the wooden chair. "Why did I leave Poland?" I repeat slowly, not sure if I heard him correctly.

He nods his head, looks straight at me.

"Poland is a Jewish graveyard, but the graves have no markers." I bite my lip. "I returned from the Nazi death camps and found no trace of my family." I take a deep breath. "Those who survived the Nazi death camps are being murdered in Poland again."

He lowers his eyes. "I am sorry. I had to ask. Sometimes Nazis enter the United States posing as Holocaust survivors, to hide their past. I am sorry. We must be careful."

Tears glide over my face. He gives my shoulder a gentle squeeze as he walks quickly out of the room.

My thoughts are back in the huge courtroom again. We have passed all the tests. We have answered all the questions. The day is finally here. "Today is the day," I whisper.

The names of the applicants are called. I hold my breath.

"Ruth Sender, formerly Ruta Senderowicz."

I stand up weakly.

"Morris Sender, formerly Moishe Senderowicz."

Moniek's eyes glow with pride.

Other names are called. We wait silently.

"Raise your right hand," says the judge.

I raise my hand. We are sworn in.

"Put your right hand over your heart. Repeat after me: I pledge allegiance to the Flag of the United States of America and to the Republic for which it stands, one nation under God, indivisible, with liberty and justice for all."

Voices around me beam loud and clear.

"With liberty and justice for all." My voice is strong, proud.

"Congratulations, new Americans!" The judge raises his voice high. "You are now citizens of the United States of America!"

Moniek and I hold each other tight. Around us people laugh, cry, shout for joy.

"Congratulations, new American," I whisper in Moniek's ear.

"Congratulations, new American." He holds me close. "We are American citizens."

28

My sister Chana and my brother Yankl are still in Canada. It has been several years since I last saw them. My sister Mala and I are in the United States. We yearn to be together, but borders and immigration laws keep us apart. We share one another's lives through letters, pictures, phone calls. I think of the long, painful years when we did not even know whether we still had a family, and I am grateful for what we have.

I remember our good-bye in 1939. The Germans had conquered Poland. Our secure world had fallen apart. Mama, a widow with seven children, was afraid for her three older children, Mala, Chana, and Yankl. She sent them across the Russian border "to safety."

I hear her words again and again. *Who will do any harm to a widow and small children? We must remain. We must hold on to our home. This will not last long. They will soon return safely.*

Could we have imagined that we would be separated for seven long years? Could we have believed that when we finally found one another, Mala, Chana, Yankl, and I would be the only survivors of our large family? Could we have believed that we would be wandering in the land that is soaked with Jewish blood for five years, searching for a place to rebuild our shattered lives? Could we have believed we would be forced to go anywhere that a door of refuge would open, and be separated again?

Five more years have passed. We are the lucky ones. We have survived. Why must we live apart?

At last. After years of waiting, after mounds of paperwork, questions and more questions, Chana and her family are permitted to emigrate from Canada to the United States of America. We gladly share our home. A short time later, Yankl and *his* family arrive.

Are we really reunited? Am I dreaming again?

29

I feel at peace as I watch our children at play. Normal, happy, healthy children. They have roots. They will have a future. But sometimes a dark shadow glides over their young faces. They miss the warmth of a grandmother's touch, the strength of a grandfather's embrace.

My son Allen cuddles softly in my lap one day. "Mommy, would it be okay to make believe that Mrs. Gruner is our grandma?" He pleads with his eyes. "I know it's only make-believe, but. . . ." He turns to his younger brother. "Mrs. Gruner likes us. Right, Harvey?"

"She really does, Mommy." Harvey agrees eagerly. "I know she's David and Peter's grandma, but she wouldn't mind having two more grandsons."

I see the hopeful glow in their young faces.

"It is only make-believe, Mommy." Allen's voice is very quiet.

My eyes well up with tears. I blink them quickly away. "Are you sure it will be okay with David and Peter? Will they want to share their grandma?"

"They will. They will," they both chime eagerly.

"And Mrs. Gruner. . . . Well, if it's okay with her."

They run quickly to the door, shouting gleefully. "Thank you, Mommy, thank you."

Through the window I watch them race toward their friends' house. Tears flow silently over my cheeks.

"Mommy, it's okay." Louie is suddenly by my side. I did not hear him enter the room.

"They're still children. It's okay to make-believe."

I hug my son. "You are only nine years old. You are also a child."

His eyes follow his little brothers as they disappear into the entrance of the huge brick building at the end of the street.

"I'm too old to make-believe." His voice is sad. I hold him close to me. Absorbed in our own thoughts, we remain silently at the window.

30

The Parent-Teacher Association at PS 32, the children's school, is very active. I take pride in working with this group. The women I get together with are dedicated to their children's education, friendly and warm.

After we finish the business at hand, we linger for a while. Often the women speak of their children's exciting visits with their grandmas and grandpas. "They spoil those kids rotten," one woman proclaims, smiling. "But what are grandparents for?"

We speak of the wisdom of our children and their many questions. I feel a tightness in my chest as I recall my children's questions.

"Why? Why did our grandparents die?" I hear Louie's voice.

"Why did the world keep silent?" Allen's puzzled eyes flash before me.

"Why don't we have any pictures of our grandparents? Why don't we have any pictures of your childhood? Daddy's childhood?" Harvey's endless questions rush through my mind.

My thoughts wander back to an evening a short time ago. My sons are getting ready for bed.

"Read to us, Mommy," Louie prompts with a twinkle in his eyes. "I know we can read by ourselves, but you do it so well."

"Flattery will get you somewhere," I reply, smiling. "How about A Child's Garden of Verses?"

"Fine."

Suddenly Harvey asks, "Did your mother read to you when you were a kid?"

The question startles me. Louie gives Harvey a stern look. "Don't ask questions that upset Mommy."

"She did when she had the time. She had to work to support her family, after my daddy died from typhus. She liked to hear me read. I always had many questions for her."

"What kinds of questions?" Louie asks.

Mama's face is vivid in my mind. " 'Why? Why are there wars? Why can't people be good to each other?'

" 'Someday . . .' she would say. You ask the same questions now. I give the same answer. Someday. . . ."

Allen touches my hand. His warm little fingers move slowly back and forth. "I wish I had known my grandparents," he says.

"Ruth Sender. Don't you agree that grandparents spoil their grandchildren?" one of the women asks, bringing me back to the discussion of the group around me.

"I wish my children were that lucky. I wish they had grandparents to spoil them."

"They have no grandparents?" she says sadly. "I am sorry."

Nettie, my neighbor, sits across from me. I feel her eyes on my face. "Ruth's family was murdered by the Nazis. She is a Holocaust survivor. The children of the survivors have no grandparents." She is angry at the Nazis. She is angry at the ignorance of the women in this group.

Heavy, painful silence suddenly fills the room. The women turn their eyes away from me.

I feel sorry for making them uncomfortable.

31

My days are filled with caring for my family, attending PTA meetings, occasionally writing poems. Poems remembering the past. Poems rejoicing in my freedom. Poems commemorating the strength of survivors to create again. Some of the poems are published in journals.

I remember the sack of straw I slept on in the concentration camps. The poems I wrote, then hid in the straw. Now my poems, too, are free.

My nights are filled with nightmares. I am forever running, forever hiding from the Nazis. In my nightmares I have three little boys with me. The little boys look like my younger brothers, but their names are the names of my three sons. I am a child, but I am also a mother. The boys are sometimes my brothers, sometimes my sons. I know I must hide them. Save them from the Nazis.

I hear the Nazis pounding at my door. I hear them shouting, "Jews, out! Jews, out!" But how can the Nazis be here? I am in America. I wake up screaming, "Not again! Not again!"

Moniek wipes the perspiration from my face, holds me tight. My nightmare remains vivid in my mind. I tremble. Cling to Moniek. We do not speak. There is no need for words.

He, too, has nightmares of the past. He, too, runs from the Nazis, fights them, screams in his sleep. I slip out of Moniek's embrace, rush to see my children. They are safely, peacefully sleeping. Softly I touch each one of them with my quivering lips. I linger for a while at their beds, then return to the safety of my husband's arms.

My heart is still pounding. I am afraid to fall asleep again. I know the nightmares will return. They always do. With eyes open wide, I wait for dawn.

Moniek twists and turns as he tries to fall back to sleep. My nightmare interrupted his rest. I feel bad. He has to get up very early.

He works in a produce market. The work is hard. The pay is low. When he returns late in the evening, tired and tense, he speaks very little. I see the anger in his eyes, hear it in his voice. He holds the bitterness and frustration bottled up within him.

"Moniek. We survived hell. We have so much to be grateful for," I remind him.

"Grateful that I work hard and we hardly manage."

"We are doing fine. Stop being angry."

He mumbles something under his breath. My eyes well up with tears. I blink them away.

The children, too, suffer. He is very strict with them. "Moniek, don't be so hard on the boys," I plead. "When they were babies you were playful, tender, loving. As they get older, you hide your feelings."

"What do you want from me?"

"We have wonderful kids. Show them that you love them."

"They know I love them."

"Why can't you tell them?"

"I will not spoil them."

"You are not spoiling them. Let them know you care."

"Someday they will understand." His voice is soft.

"But what about today? What about now, Moniek?"

"Who am I working for now, if not for them?" He raises his voice.

"You will wake the children."

"One has to be strict with boys," he whispers hoarsely.

"You are wrong."

Now, cuddling silently with him, I recall our muffled, often repeated arguments.

The morning rays fall softly over his face. His mouth is twisted in a painful grimace. I wipe my tears.

My heart goes out to him. My heart goes out to my children.

32

I sit across from Moniek at the kitchen table. The children are outside. The house is quiet.

For days I have been telling myself I must wait for the right moment to share my plans with my husband. I know he will not be pleased with what I want to do. But you will have to face it sooner or later, a little voice within me whispers. So do it.

I feel nervous. "I want to go to the Jewish Teachers Seminary." The words I have rehearsed carefully again and again rush from my mouth now. "I've always wanted to be a teacher of Jewish history and culture." I keep my eyes glued to his face. "I'm sure it will not be easy, but I want to do it, Moniek."

He stares at me. "You want to become a teacher?"

"I can get a scholarship to cover the tuition. It will not be a financial burden, Moniek."

"But you are a mother of three young children." His voice is filled with anger and disbelief. "A mother belongs at home."

"I know I am a mother. I love being a mother. I could go to school part-time." I try to control the sudden anger within me.

"This is crazy! You've lost your mind!"

"I can do it, Moniek." My voice is strong.

His mouth tightens. "When will you go to classes?"

"In the evening. You are home in the evening."

He studies my face as if seeing me for the first time. His eyes flash angrily. "What about dinner? When will the children eat?"

"I will feed the kids before I go."

He walks away from the table, stops at the window for a moment, then sits down again.

"This is crazy," he murmurs. "This is crazy."

"Maybe . . . but I must try."

We sit silently for a while.

"Where is the seminary?" he asks suddenly.

"In Manhattan."

"In Manhattan!" he shouts. "It takes one hour each way by subway from here to Manhattan. You are crazy!"

"Moniek, I do not want to upset you like this." My eyes feel moist. "Please . . . do not make it hard on me."

He stands up again. Paces back and forth angrily. Stops in front of me. "What do you need this for?"

"My life was torn apart, my dreams destroyed. But I must try again."

He stares silently at the window. I take his hand in mine. "You work hard. Look at it from a practical point of view. When I become a teacher and the kids are older, I will be able to help."

"I can still support you all."

"Moniek." I press his hand tightly. "I know you can support us."

"So what do you need this for?" he demands.

"It is not the money." I blink away the tears in my eyes. "I always wanted to teach, to write."

"I still think you've lost your mind." His voice has lost its edge.

"Could be."

I feel drained. I rest my head on the table. "I will not know until I try."

"We will think about it," Moniek replies softly.

"Good." I raise my head, straighten my back. "Good."

33

I sit in a classroom at the Jewish Teachers Seminary. My eyes wander around the room, studying carefully the pictures of famous Jewish personalities covering the walls. They bring back my childhood, my school days.

Am I really here? In my ears ring Moniek's words, "You've lost your mind." Before me flash the puzzled, yet excited, faces of my three sons as they wave good-bye to Mommy, leaving for school. This is a new experience for all of us.

I study the faces of the students around me. They range from young adults to middle-aged people. Are they as nervous as I am? I wonder.

The classroom door opens. An elderly man, medium height, hair woven with gray, enters the classroom. His mild eyes gaze softly at the mixture of new students before him. "I am Mr. Kazdan."

Chills run down my spine. My heart pounds. Mr. Kazdan? As a child I was in awe of this man, the head of the Jewish schools in Poland. I was one of the thousands of children in the Jewish school system. He has changed so much. He looks old and tired.

Of Jewish life in Poland, only ashes are left. The school system we loved, he as a prominent educator, I as a young student dreaming of becoming an educator, is no more. We survived. Here we are. He is still teaching. I am still pursuing my dream.

I swallow hard. Raise my hand. My voice shakes. "Mr. Kazdan. I am from Lodz. A graduate of the Medem school."

He stares wide-eyed. "One of my surviving children." His voice cracks. "What is your name?"

"My maiden name is Riva Minska. I am the niece of Baruch Grundman."

His eyes well up with tears. "Baruch Grundman? My Baruch? I took so much pride in him. A student of my schools who became a teacher and returned to teach at the same school he came from. Such a dedicated educator. Such a talented artist. Such a wonderful human being."

He moves closer to me.

"Did he survive?"

"No," I reply hoarsely. "No."

He turns. His shoulders drop as if crushed by a sudden weight. He remains silent for a while, then turns to the class once again. His eyes move slowly from student to student. "We are here to perpetuate Jewish education by becoming teachers. A hard task. An important task. A thousand years of Jewish culture, Jewish life in Eastern Europe lies in ashes."

His burning eyes hang on my face. "We must remember."

He turns to a young student in the corner of the room. "We must learn."

His voice takes on strength. "We must teach."

34

The subway ride to the seminary takes about an hour. I prop my books on my lap and begin to do homework. I like my work. Still, my eyes wander from my books to the people around me. I search their faces. Is that a familiar glance, a gesture I have seen before? Is the man sitting across from me someone from my childhood? Why is he looking at me? Do I remind him of someone he has known? I stare at him. He lowers his head and begins to read his newspaper. I slump, dejected, in my seat.

I fantasize. I sit on a train. Suddenly a tired, middle-aged woman sits down across from me. She looks at me. Our eyes meet. We fall into each other's embrace, sobbing. "My child, my child," she cries. "I have searched for you all these years. . . ." I bump into a stranger in the street. I turn to apologize for my clumsiness. He grabs me in his arms, shouting, "Riva, it is I, Motele, your brother. I survived. Moishele survived. I'll take you to him." I look around me. Am I crazy? Hoping against hope.

I listen for the sound of familiar voices in trains, in streets, in stores. I dream the impossible.

The sound of German makes me shiver. A group of tourists, smiling, with cameras on their shoulders, enters the train. My heart beats fast.

Who are they? Do they know where my family is? Are they murderers?

I stare at their faces. The older couple is about the right age to have been my guards. I stare at the young people in the group and wonder, did they ever hear the word *Holocaust?* Is the past kept a dark secret from them?

Have they been raised with lies about the past of their grandparents, their parents?

I feel no hatred toward the young generation. I think of my children. They, too, know little about the past.

How will we tell our children? The question posed by a survivor in a displaced persons camp years ago keeps demanding an answer. How do we share our pain?

Moniek and I speak very little about the past. Are we protecting our children? I am not sure. I know of survivors who tell and retell the horrors of the past. How will this affect their children? I wish we knew what was right.

My oldest child, Laibele, is almost thirteen. Soon he will be bar mitzvah, a full-fledged member of the Jewish people. If only he had grandparents, as other children have, to share this day.

Tears glide slowly down my cheeks. I ignore the puzzled look of the lady next to me. My thoughts turn back to my children.

Students of a Jewish supplementary school, the Workmen's Circle, they learn about their heritage. Laibele has completed five years and is about to graduate. He recites

Yiddish poems he has learned at the Jewish school. He recites a poem about a heroic Jewish teacher in a ghetto of Poland. Surrounded by death, she continued to teach. She shared her spiritual strength with her young students.

Now, in a New York subway, surrounded by strangers, I see the ruins of the ghetto. I see the secret classroom. I feel the agony of the teacher. I hear the words of the poem:

> The children,
> They are coming.
> She counts them.
> Oh, better not count,
> Twenty perished last night.

Faces flash before my eyes. Faces of my teachers. Faces of my classmates. We were twenty-seven young, blossoming saplings, full of hope for the future. Only four survived.

I sigh painfully. The woman next to me stares at me again for a moment, then turns her head toward the window.

I close my eyes. My children's smiling faces appear before me. A warm, joyous feeling enfolds me.

We, their parents, survived Hitler's master plan to annihilate the Jewish people. Scorched by the flames of death, we rose again. We are here. A new Jewish generation is here.

35

Mr. Kazdan, my seminary teacher, is very impressed with my schoolwork. "It shows that you have a strong Jewish background." He smiles softly. "I am glad that we, the educators of your childhood, did not fail you." Faces of my teachers float before my eyes, smiling proudly. *We did not fail you.* They all died, but their faces, their voices live in my heart.

Mr. Kazdan walks slowly toward his desk, picks up pages of notebook paper. All eyes are on his face. He looks from the paper toward me. "Your essays are wonderful. You speak of a strong tree, an old tree, uprooted by a terrible storm. You speak of tiny, surviving branches coming to life again. Your words flow like poetry."

He stares at the pages in his hands. "They should be published. Send them to a Yiddish newspaper."

"I did." My face feels hot. "I did . . . but . . . they rejected them."

His eyes flash with anger. "I'll do it. I know the editors."

He sends a story to *Freie Arbeiter Stimme,* a Yiddish newspaper. They print it. Mr. Kazdan proudly passes around copies of the newspaper.

I mention to him my poetry written in the concentration camp. He is eager to read it. He is very moved. "I wish I could find someone to publish it." He sighs. "But even if we write editorial notes with the poems, only the ones who were there will understand." He stares into the distance. "They are not the ones who need to read your poems . . . and the rest of the world does not want to listen. They want to forget."

You must remember! You must remember! I see the hollow eyes of the girls in the concentration camps again. *We must tell the world.* I lower my head.

"The world does not want to listen." I repeat Mr. Kazdan's words.

He picks up my chin gently. "Do not give up."

I wonder if anyone will ever read them. I wonder if they will ever do some good.

I mention my poems to my children's Jewish school teacher, David Berezer. We speak often of the past as I help out at the school. He, too, comes from Lodz, Poland, but he was one of the lucky ones who left Poland before World War II. He lost many members of his family. "I feel guilty that I left them behind," he says. Tears flow over his face.

"I feel guilty that I survived," I whisper. "I feel guilty that my poems, the witnesses of horror, degradation, hope, stay buried in a drawer, silent, useless."

"May I please read them, Mrs. Sender?"

"They will make you cry."

"I cry every day."

I bring him the poems. He touches them with quivering hands. His lips move silently as he reads them. His face becomes a mask of pain. "You are the living Anne Frank." He takes my hand in his. "She wrote in hiding. You wrote in concentration camps. You both held on to hope."

He wipes the tears from his face. "I want to send your poems to the Institute of Jewish Research. They are valuable testimony to the strength of the human spirit."

I make copies. He gives them to the institute, YIVO.

"At least they will not be hidden in my drawer." I sigh. But will anyone read them? Will anyone learn from them?

A small voice in the back of my mind tells me to persist.

36

"Slowly pass days, years fly by fast." The phrase takes on more meaning as the years go by. The children are growing so fast. Louie is applying for college. Allen is in high school, Harvey in junior high. They are all bright, intelligent, warm human beings. Moniek and I take much pride in them. They make life worth living.

I marvel at the miracle. In spite of our suffering, in spite of our constant nightmares, we manage to raise a loving, sensitive family. My head fills with voices coming from the darkness of the concentration camp barrack. *We must live. We must survive to take revenge for our torment.*

"This is our revenge." My lips move silently. "Children capable of laughter. Children capable of compassion. Children capable of love. This is our revenge."

Our small circle of friends are all survivors. We feel comfortable with one another. No need to explain sudden sighs, sudden tears. No need to describe a ghetto, a labor camp, a death camp. Bound by unspoken words, by invisible threads, we are one another's family now. We are one another's strength. The agony of the concentration camps brought us together. Memories of our vanished world hold us together.

At our survivors' meetings we recall the past, our lost

families, our vanished world. At our homes we plan the future. College. Professional goals. Contributions to humanity.

37

My neighbor Nettie puts her empty coffee cup on the table. The kids are at school, and we have our morning coffee together before she leaves on her daily trip to the local library.

"Nettie, when do you find time to read all those books?" I gaze at the shopping cart filled with books, which she left at the door. "You must be inhaling the books. You are unbelievable."

"Well." She shrugs her shoulders. "I read fast. I do not have your talents. You can write. You teach. So I make up for it by reading."

"You are a walking encyclopedia." I pour fresh coffee into her cup. "I am in awe of you."

She shrugs her shoulders again and changes the topic. We speak of school activities, children. "Ruth, I see that most of the children of survivors work hard in school. They strive for medicine, law, social work, teaching. But my sons, Steven and Michael, speak of outer space, of exploring other worlds."

She sighs. "Steven lives in another world. My husband is a teacher, I am an avid reader, and still I cannot get him interested in books."

We sit silently for a while, staring at our coffee, searching for answers.

The children of survivors. Nettie's words pound in my ears.

I break the long silence. "The children of survivors, even if they do not speak about it, feel the hidden agony of their parents. I think that in their own way they, too, are survivors."

I take a deep breath. "Many are searching for a world of justice to make up for the injustices we suffered. They work hard so that they can reach their professional goals to help those in need of help."

Nettie takes my hand in hers.

"They are carrying a heavy burden, Nettie. Each child of survivors is named after someone who perished. Grandparents who were murdered while we, their parents, were still children. Aunts and uncles who were murdered as children and never had the chance to live."

My voice breaks, "Maybe we, the survivors, expect our children to make up our losses, and they try to make us happy by working hard, by excelling."

Nettie caresses my hand softly. "Do the children of survivors show emotional problems, Ruth?"

"I am sure some do. I know of very few."

There is a sudden anger in my voice. "There are those who are not survivors, or children of survivors, who have emotional problems, too, Nettie."

"I did not mean to upset you, Ruth. I'm sorry." She picks up her cup, holds it without drinking, puts it down again. "I often wonder how you managed to live through such hell. I wonder how the survivors remained normal. Remained human."

I gaze at Nettie. "What is normal? If sitting at the window with your heart pounding until your child comes into view is normal . . . I am normal. If trying to hide children from the Nazis in your nightmares, children who are sometimes your little brothers, sometimes your sons, is normal . . . I am normal. If waking up screaming and rushing to see if your children are safely in their beds is normal . . . I am normal."

She lowers her eyes.

We stare silently into the cold coffee in our cups.

38

June 1964. We are in our new home in Commack, Long Island, a suburb of New York. Away from the noisy and crowded city streets.

Is this real? The house is bright, sunny, spacious. I close my eyes and see the wooden planks in the cubicles of the concentration camp that were home to me, then open my eyes again quickly. It is real. It is real. As long as there is life, there is hope.

The warm rays of sunlight caress my face. Birds sing on the window ledge. A home at last.

Moniek's job as produce manager at a supermarket brought us out here. He looks happy puttering in the fresh earth in the yard, planting a tree. He comes from a small town in Poland. His childhood was spent among trees. Somehow that young tree he is planting now seems to be his link to the past.

He turns to his sons. His voice has a special, joyous ring. "Boys, you should have seen me climbing the tallest trees in the orchards of Wyszogrod. There was not a tree too tall for me."

Louie, Allen, Harvey, busy pulling weeds from the yard, smile slightly, trying somehow to visualize their father climbing trees.

I look at Moniek, remember the young, muscular man whom I met at a water pump in Wroclaw, remember the ease with which he worked the iron water pump. For me it is easy to see him climbing the tallest trees in the orchards of Wyszogrod.

"Ruth." Moniek puts down the shovel near the newly planted tree, pleased with his accomplishment. "We will plant a cherry tree, an apple tree, a pear tree."

"Are we planting an orchard?" I smile, seeing the glow in his eyes. "I want a lilac bush."

"You'll get your lilac bush, too."

"It will take years until we see it blossom."

"So. We are not going anywhere. This is home."

"This is home," I whisper softly. "We came a long way from concentration camps, displaced persons camps, to a home of our own.

"It would be wonderful if my sisters, my brother, and their families, too, moved out here, but their jobs keep them in the city. And I will miss Karola and Nettie. . . ." My voice trails off sadly.

"We would like it, too." Louie's brown eyes glide softly over my face. "But they can all visit. It's not that far."

Nagging thoughts come and go. Should I have remained in the city to be closer to my sisters and brother? Will we manage the bills? Will Moniek's salary sustain us? We had to borrow money to make the down payment for the house.

"We will manage. We will manage." Moniek chases my worries.

"Do you realize that we do not even have a bankbook, Moniek? It makes me feel insecure."

He stares at me. "I'll see what I can do," he mumbles under his breath.

Two days later he hands me an envelope.

"What is it, Moniek?" I hold the envelope in my hands without opening it.

"Open it and see," he urges.

Slowly I open the envelope. "A bankbook?"

"I got paid today. It is only a ten-dollar account, but if it will make you feel secure. . . ." He grins.

I look at the little book in my hand. "My security blanket." I lower my eyes. "It may sound silly, but we all need a security blanket sometimes."

My sons play ball after school in our spacious backyard. No more playing ball on the city street, rushing to the side each time a car approaches, my heart skipping a beat at the sound of screeching car wheels.

A child in the next-door yard laughs happily as she swings high on her swing. This is a place for a child to enjoy the pleasures of childhood in comfort.

Moniek reads my thoughts as we hear the happy sounds of the children around us.

39

"Moniek." My voice quivers lightly as I take Moniek's hand in mine. "You are going to be the father of a new baby."

A big grin covers his face. He pulls me close to him. Holds me tight. "I am very, very happy." His eyes glow. "I am very, very happy."

I put my head on his shoulder. "How will the boys take it?" I wonder aloud. "Louie is in college, Allen and Harvey in high school. How will they react to the news?" My voice betrays my nervousness.

"It will be okay, sweetheart. It is great news. A new baby." His voice cracks. "I am so very happy."

"Me, too." I whisper softly. "Me, too."

All during dinner Moniek and I exchange mysterious glances. I notice Louie watching us, puzzled.

"Is there something going on that we don't know about? You're both acting kind of strange." His voice is low. "What is it?"

Moniek looks from one to the other, smiling. "How would you like to have a baby sister or brother?"

My heart beats fast. I gaze at my sons. Their baffled eyes dart from Moniek to me.

"You're not kidding?" Louie exclaims.

"No. We are not kidding," I reply softly.

Their faces light up. "Mazel tov." Louie puts his arms around me.

"I hope it's a girl," Allen says, beaming.

"We have to think of names," Harvey proclaims happily. "A name is important."

"Thank you, boys." My eyes fill with tears. "I was afraid of how you would react." I blink away the tears. "I should have known that you would welcome the good news."

"What about a name?" Harvey persists. "You can't stick a baby with a terrible name for the rest of its life."

"It would be nice to have a little sister now," Allen declares wistfully.

"Yes. But if it's a boy, that will be fine, too," Louie says. "Are you okay?" He turns to me. "Did you see the doctor?"

"I am fine." I take a deep breath. "If it is a girl, her Yiddish name will be Nacha, after my mother." I swallow hard. "If it is a boy, we will use a masculine version of Nacha. I don't have to tell you that we Jews name our children after relatives who have died. Louie is named after Daddy's father, whose Yiddish name was Laibl." I stop. "I also had a brother, Laibl. He died in the ghetto."

They watch me silently. I clear my voice. "Allen is named after my father, whose Yiddish name was Avrom.

Harvey is named after Daddy's mother. Her Yiddish name was Chava. The masculine version is Chaim."

I swallow the lump in my throat. "Now my mother, too, will have a namesake."

I see dark shadows appear in their eyes. Each time the past comes up, the dark shadows fill their eyes. We sit silently for a moment.

"We know then that the name will begin with the letter *n*." Harvey breaks the silence. "Let's think of *n* names for girls."

"What if it is a boy?" I smile.

"No. It will be a girl." Moniek grins.

"Whichever it is, let it be healthy." I gaze with pride and joy at my three sons. "And it is a lucky baby to have three wonderful guys like you for brothers."

They shrug their shoulders. The shadows in their eyes vanish.

"A boy or a girl. Just let it be healthy," I whisper softly.

40

September 17, 1966. I am half asleep. I feel my nose tickled. "What a pesky fly," I mumble with my eyes closed. I try to push it away. The tickling continues. I touch my face again and feel a warm hand in mine. I open my eyes slowly.

Before me stands Moniek. His face is radiant, his voice beaming. "Wake up, sleepyhead. We have a daughter."

I stare at the smiling face bending over me. "Where am I?" I ask, dazed.

"You are at the hospital." He caresses my hand softly. "Wake up." His voice sounds far away.

"Wake up. You had a little girl. We have a daughter, sweetheart."

"We do?" My eyes close heavily.

"Yes. We do." Moniek bends over me.

Suddenly I am wide awake. "We do?"

"We do! We do!" he shouts joyously.

"We do?" I stare at the nurse standing by my bed. "I do not believe it."

"Nurse." Moniek turns to the woman. "Please bring in the baby."

"Please, let her sleep." She sounds annoyed with him.

"The doctor gave her something to help her rest after the baby was born. She is not awake yet. Let her rest."

"Bring the baby, please," Moniek pleads.

"New fathers," she mumbles as she leaves.

My mind is beginning to clear. "Moniek, I remember the doctor telling me, 'It is a girl, Ruth' before I floated away. I thought it was a dream."

Moniek squeezes my hand lovingly. "It is no dream. Everything went well. We have a daughter."

The nurse returns, holding a small pink bundle in her arms. "Here is your little girl, Ruth," she says, putting the baby on my chest.

I stare in amazement. My child. My little girl. She opens her eyes, looks straight at me. "She knows me, Moniek. She knows I am her mother." My eyes fill with tears.

"She cannot see yet," the nurse mumbles.

"Yes, she can," I insist as I quickly unfold the blanket the baby is wrapped in.

The nurse objects. "What are you doing, Ruth? Don't undress the baby."

"I just want to see if she has ten fingers, ten toes."

The nurse smiles for the first time. "You new mothers, you're impossible. This is your first baby, right?"

"We have three wonderful sons." My voice rings with pride. "We have three wonderful sons."

"This is your first daughter. No wonder you two act the way you do. Congratulations." Her voice has lost its formal tone. "I'm very happy for you." She leaves the room grinning broadly.

Moniek sits down at the edge of the bed. His eyes glow. "All went well. The doctor said you are both fine. How are you feeling?"

"Fine, Moniek. I am so happy." My fingers caress the soft little hands of the baby. "She looks so small." I kiss her head gently.

Moniek grins. "She is not breakable, sweetheart. You can hold her."

"I forgot how small newborn babies are. It has been a long time." I pick her up in my arms. "Nachele. Your name is Nachele—Nancy," I whisper. "My mother's name has been passed on to you, my child." Tears glide over my face.

Moniek watches silently. "The names of our parents have been passed on, Moniek. Our children carry the names of the grandparents they never knew."

Moniek turns his eyes toward the window, then turns back toward me again. He clears his throat. "The boys are overjoyed." A smile appears on his face. "They are calling all their friends with the wonderful news."

"When will they be here? I can't wait to see them." I, too, smile.

"They will come right after classes. They are eager to see you and their sister. Oh, yes. Your brother-in-law, Yosef, sent a message."

"What is the message?"

"Well." He laughs. "He said he will not believe it is a girl until he checks it out himself. He does not take anyone's word for it."

"Does he want a doctor's certificate?" I, too, laugh. "I am sure he will check it out."

The nurse returns to take the baby to the nursery. "I will bring her back later. Don't look so sad. You will take her home soon. Bring the baby's clothes."

"We have no baby's clothes yet," I reply softly.

She stares at me, bewildered. "You did not prepare a baby layette?"

"It is the custom of the Jews of Eastern Europe not to buy a layette until the baby has arrived."

"Why? I assume you are Jews from Eastern Europe."

"It is meant to prevent the further pain of having to look at a layette if something goes wrong."

"Oh." She sighs heavily. "It must be agony for those parents."

"The baby will not go home naked." Moniek smiles. "There are many stores. I am sure we will get everything we need quickly. Our neighbor has a crib to lend us for a while."

"I'm sure you'll manage just fine." She walks toward the door, then turns. "It's interesting to learn of other people's customs."

41

We live in a quiet, peaceful neighborhood. The trees planted only a few years ago are blossoming, their many branches reaching toward the blue sky. I watch the young children playing with Nancy. They, too, blossom.

My neighbors, warm, friendly, join me in front of the house. We sit in comfortable chairs, watching the children roll happily in the grass. We chat quietly.

The conversation turns from children to grandparents. "My mother checks every day on her grandson," one says, sighing heavily. The annoyance in her voice sends chills down my spine.

"I know what you mean." Another nods her head slowly. "Our parents think we can't raise our children without their guidance."

"Maybe they just want to be part of their grandchildren's lives." My eyes glide slowly over Nancy's smiling face. "Let them have that pleasure."

"They live in a different world. Their views are old-fashioned."

I say nothing.

"What do you do when your mother acts like an over-protective grandmother, Ruth? How do you handle it?"

My head spins. I gasp for breath.

The woman looks at me. "You're so pale, Ruth. Are you okay?"

I wipe the cold sweat from my face.

"What's wrong?"

"Do you feel sick?"

"Is there anything we can do?"

My neighbors' worried voices sound far away. Slowly my head clears.

"When you're sick, it's good to have a mother to lend a hand," one woman says, putting a glass of cold water before me. "Does your mother live far from here, Ruth?"

I stare into the distance. I hear the children's happy voices around me. "I have no mother."

"I'm sorry. I didn't know." Her eyes reflect her pity. "She must have died young."

I nod silently.

"What did she die of?" Her eyes remain curiously on my face.

I press my hands tightly together. "She was gassed by the Nazis." The words come slowly, painfully.

I hear a horrified gasp.

"She died because she was a Jew." I sip the cold water

slowly. Take a deep breath. "My children have no grand-parents. They were all murdered by the Nazis."

Stricken eyes hang frozen on my face.

"I'm sorry." I hear the soft voice of a neighbor. "How could we know?"

"You never speak of it," another adds gently.

I stare at the bright sun in the blue sky. "And the sun did not stop shining," I whisper.

Holding a yellow dandelion in her little hands, Nancy rushes, smiling, toward me. "I picked a pretty flower for you, Mommy."

I take her in my arms. Hold her tight.

42

You never speak about it. My neighbor's voice echoes in my ears as I pull from the drawer a piece I wrote, long ago, about life in the ghetto cage. The piece was rejected by *Reader's Digest.*

"The Cage." I read the title of my unpublished story. "I must try again," I whisper slowly. "I must try again."

Before me is a copy of *Hadassah* magazine. April 1968. The date on the magazine looms large before my eyes. April 1968. Suddenly another April date flashes in my mind. April 1943. "The Warsaw ghetto uprising," I whisper as I stare at the date before me.

It is twenty-five years since the remnants of the Jews of the ghetto of Warsaw, Poland, rose up in armed resistance against the Nazis. With only a few secretly obtained guns, they took their last stand against the powerful German weapons. It took courage. It took strength.

I see the starved eyes of my little brothers. *We, too, resisted,* they persist. *We held on to life as long as we could. Each day we survived was resistance. Remember! Remember! Remember!*

I take paper from the desk and write.

Dear *Hadassah* Editor:

It is now 25 years since the Warsaw ghetto uprising. I spent my teenage years in the ghetto of Lodz, in Auschwitz, and in other camps. I am enclosing herewith an episode of my life in the ghetto of Lodz to honor those gentle souls who tried in their own way to fight for honor and dignity. My three brothers did not survive. Laibele died in the ghetto. Motele and Moishele were transported with me to Auschwitz. They did not come back.

Ruth Minsky Sender

I attach the letter to the pages of my story, put them into a brown envelope, carefully copy the address of the magazine. I rush to the mailbox on the street corner, before I can change my mind, and toss it in.

Several days later, the phone rings. A man introduces himself as a *Hadassah* magazine editor. "Ruth Minsky Sender, a more fitting memorial to the heroes of the Warsaw ghetto would be hard to find."

"You are going to publish my story?" My heart beats like a drum.

"We will be honored."

43

My three sons hug me. Kiss me. They have read the piece in *Hadassah* magazine. I feel their agony. I feel their distress.

"You never speak about it." Louie utters the words softly, holds me tight.

"I cannot speak about it. When I write, I cry. Sometimes my tears soak the paper. Still, I keep going." I gaze sadly at the thoughtful, loving faces of my sons. "I know I should speak. But . . . the words choke me." I see tears in their eyes.

"Is it better if we don't ask questions?" Allen holds my hand tightly. "There are so many questions we want to ask."

I search for an answer.

"I always ask questions. Am I hurting you and Daddy?" Harvey asks softly. He looks at Louie and Allen. "It's so frustrating."

They nod silently.

"It hurts if we speak," I say. "It hurts if we do not speak."

"When we ask sometimes about"—Louie looks away—"about the past . . . your answer is short and you quickly change the subject. Daddy just keeps silent."

"He is hoping, as do many survivors, that if he does not speak about the past, it will be easier to forget."

"Can he forget?"

I shake my head silently.

"I thought he keeps silent because he's tough," Allen comments softly.

"He hides behind his tough, rugged appearance, my son."

"But our questions need answers," Harvey insists.

When my sons were young, it was easier not to answer. But they are not small children anymore. They are sensitive, intelligent adults. My heart fills with pride.

"It is hard, very hard, for survivors to answer their sons and daughters. For some harder than others."

I see the dejected look in their eyes.

"We are trying to spare our children. . . ."

Silence. Painful silence fills the air.

Louie and Judy, the girl he will soon marry, sit in the living room that evening. I am in the kitchen. I hear their subdued voices.

"Louie," Judy says, "I read *Hadassah* magazine." She stops. "What do I say to your mother?"

"Don't say anything, Judy," I hear him say. "My mother understands."

44

My world is collapsing. Allen has been drafted into the army. The threat of his being sent to Vietnam hangs heavily over our heads.

I cry a lot. Sleep very little. I live in constant fear of losing him. Still I hope. Maybe he will remain stationed in the United States. Each time I see TV pictures of our American boys dying in Vietnam, I become hysterical. I speak to Allen on the phone. My heart pounds. "Did they issue orders for you?"

"Not yet." He sounds nervous. "I'm training in radio communications. I don't know where they'll send me."

"As long as it is not over there."

There is sudden silence at the other end of the line. "I'll be home on furlough as soon as my training is finished. I can't wait to see you all."

"Neither can we. I can't wait to put my arms around you again."

The day is finally here. Allen walks into the house in his military uniform. My heart skips a beat. My son a soldier. . . .

I rush toward him, put my arms around him. He twitches. Pain fills his face. I stare at him as my knees buckle under me.

"I had some shots." He tries to avoid my gaze.

"Oh, no!" I gasp. "You have orders for overseas." Those who have orders for overseas duty are given shots against tropical diseases.

He nods silently.

My head spins. I sit down.

"I didn't want to tell you over the phone. I told Louie and Harvey."

Louie, looking very pale, nods.

"We wanted to put off telling you for as long as possible."

I feel as if the earth has just opened up under me again. I am being pulled into darkness. I put my head on the table.

Allen softly, silently caresses my hair.

I spend the night crying. Moniek stares into the darkness. I tremble as I move closer to him. He puts his arms around me silently.

"When they took Mama away, my world was covered

by darkness. My little brothers and I huddled together and cried. Then . . . we went on. Moniek, we cannot just give up. We have to do something to save our son."

He sighs. "There is nothing you can do. He has orders."

"There must be something, someone. . . ."

He remains silent.

The phone rings early in the morning.

"How are you, Mom? Louie and I were worried about you. How are you doing?" It is Louie's wife, my daughter-in-law, Judy.

"I cry a lot, Judy. I feel so helpless. Still there must be something I can do. How much pain can we endure in our lives?"

"You've endured enough pain for many lifetimes."

There is silence.

"There must be something I can do," I whisper.

"Mom." Judy raises her voice. "Maybe you should call Congressman Otis Pike. He's our congressman, and he's on the Armed Services Committee. I've heard that he's a compassionate man. Speak to him."

"Will he listen?"

"Speak to him," she insists.

"Judy." I try to hold back my tears. "I do not think I can speak to anyone without going to pieces."

"Mom, how about writing a telegram?" She sounds excited. "I'll call it in. And let's send it not only to

Congressman Pike, but also to President Nixon and to the New York senators Jacob Javits and Charles Godell."

I feel her excitement. "We must try. This is what I want to say, Judy: 'Dear Sir: Please help. We spent our childhoods in German concentration camps. Our families were murdered by the Germans. Now our son Allen Sender is being ordered to Vietnam on October 6, 1970. You could not save our families. Please help us save our son. Thank you. Ruth and Morris Sender.' "

"Okay, Mom." She hangs up quickly.

Moniek stares at me in disbelief. "You are both crazy. No one cares." He wipes his eyes quickly as he turns his head toward the window.

45

The phone rings the next day. The woman on the phone introduces herself. "I'm Congressman Pike's secretary. We received your telegram. Congressman Pike would like to speak to Allen Sender."

I hold my breath as I motion for Allen to answer the phone. I watch Allen's eyes. There is a spark of hope in them. They also look moist.

"He sounds like he cares." He clears his voice. "He

wants us to write letters to President Nixon. We're to ask for compassionate reassignment."

He looks at our flushed faces. "I think it's a waste of time. Orders are orders."

"Allen. We must try," I plead. "We cannot give up."

He shrugs his shoulders and writes. He hands me the paper when he has finished.

My eyes rush quickly past the first lines, in which he gives his rank and number and asks for compassionate reassignment. "The reason I am filing for this action is to keep my parents from suffering anymore in their lives due to war."

I feel tightness in my chest. I read on.

My parents' entire lives have been built around their children. There are a total of four children in my family. The oldest, twenty-four, was put through college by my parents and is now married. My other brother, twenty, is now in college and is being supported by my parents. I myself am in the service, and the only one living at home is my four-year-old sister. The many years of hardship my parents went through during the war show on their bodies. My father, who was wounded while in a concentration camp, still receives a small payment from the German government. My father's back trouble is also a result of his years of suffering. My mother was not left out of the hardship. She has lost partial use of her right hand due to a blood infection she contracted while in a concentration camp. Her eyes are badly damaged. She is now suffering from diabetes and a heart condition. Her nerves have not been good since her earlier suffering, and now that she has found out about my army orders, she is on the verge of a nervous breakdown.

I could not begin to tell you the full extent of their suffering, for that is something they try not to talk about. All I know is that these two people have suffered enough already for many lifetimes. I therefore ask you to consider this request for compassionate reassignment and decide on it as you must.

Allen watches me silently. I take him in my arms. He wipes the tears from my face. "I did my part," he whispers.

I look at Moniek. "It is a waste of time," he mumbles.

"We must try, Moniek."

"You write. You know what to say." He moves like a caged animal. "I will sign it."

My hands tremble. I write:

Dear President Nixon:
    Please help us. Help us. We lived a life of

hell that has never stopped hurting us. Day and night our nightmare is within us, eating our minds and bodies.

I, Morris Sender, was born in Poland in 1922. I was seventeen when the Germans marched over Poland and started murdering my people. I am the only survivor of a very large family. My father and mother, my brothers and other loved ones were killed: shot or gassed. In 1940 I was sent to Auschwitz, where I spent my youth at hard labor, starved, tortured, watching the smoke coming from death chambers' chimneys.

I do not know how I found the strength and will to live. But I survived. I survived to try to start a new life, but Auschwitz never left me. I was left with physical and mental scars that will not let me forget. I have a family, now, that my wife, Ruth, and I live for. We both lived through the same hell. We try not to talk about it, but our hell is within us, and when things go wrong our walls collapse upon us. Please help us. Please do not bring us more suffering. Please do not add to our hell and tortures by sending our son to Vietnam. Please do not fail us.

With deepest thanks,
Morris Sender

"It is a waste. It is a waste," he mutters as he signs the letter.

I take a deep breath and write my own plea.

Dear President Nixon:

Please help us and show your compassion for us and our child. I, Ruth Sender, was thirteen years old when my childhood was turned into hell and endless pain. I saw my loved ones murdered and all of our lives destroyed.

I was caged in the Polish ghetto of Lodz, where starvation and disease helped the Germans to destroy us. I saw my mother being dragged away during a German raid while she was trying to save her child from death. I never saw her again, alive or dead. There is not a trace of her or any of my loved ones. Not even the knowledge of where or how they were murdered. Sometimes I try to believe that maybe somewhere in this big world there is someone alive, looking for me, just as I am still looking for them. Our tragedy has never ended. I went through Auschwitz and several other concentration camps—from hell to hell. I tried to save my little brothers, whom I had to be both mother and father to. It was all in vain. I survived, but physically and mentally broken. We left the concentration camps, but the pain and hell of it never left us.

The roof of our new home in a free land is about to collapse on us. *Please. Please. Please.* Don't let it happen. Don't let them take our son to Vietnam.

Ruth Sender

I feel drained. I close my eyes. My lips whisper a silent prayer.

The letters mailed, we wait, we hope. A letter from Congressman Pike arrives the next day.

Dear Mr. and Mrs. Sender:

Confirming a telephone conversation with your son today, please be assured that I have contacted the appropriate military authorities relative to a possible compassionate reassignment for Allen. I have given your son the necessary information and hope that he will take appropriate action without delay so that his request will be given immediate consideration.

With best wishes and awaiting further word from your son, I am

Cordially,
Otis G. Pike

"Somebody cares. Somebody cares." I sob.

I few days later, the phone rings. I answer. It is the office of the president of the United States calling. I hold my breath as the man on the phone gives me his name and military rank. "Mrs. Sender, I was instructed to inform you that we received your telegram and your letters." He sounds very formal. "Also that Congressman Pike came by to urge immediate action." His voice softens. "I wish you the best of luck. I would like to speak to your son, SP/4 Allen Sender."

I hand Allen the telephone. I watch his face as he listens intently to the man on the phone. He sits still for a moment, then hangs up the phone.

"I don't believe I just spoke to the office of the commander in chief of the armed forces." He catches his breath. "He said that while they are considering my request, my orders for Vietnam are on hold. Not to report anywhere until I hear from them. Do I dare hope?"

"We must hope. We must."

Every time there is a knock at the door, every time the phone rings, we all jump. We wait, hearts pounding, different thoughts racing through our tired minds.

"Will they have compassion?"

"What will happen if they deny our plea?"

"Could something happen if he remains home past October 6, 1970, when he is due to report for duty?"

The phone rings. It is for Allen: the office of the commander in chief of the armed forces. There is deadly silence in the room. All eyes are on Allen. I try to read the expression on my son's face. His eyes remain tense.

"Yes, sir. Thank you, sir," are the only words he utters.

We stare silently at him. He takes a deep breath. "My orders for Vietnam have been canceled. I will receive new orders." He stops. "I am going to Korea."

He gazes at me, his eyes moist. "It is far away. But . . . it is not Vietnam."

46

"*A yingele. A maydele.* A little boy. A little girl." In a bright, sunny classroom, twenty-two young voices repeat slowly after me a Yiddish children's song. Once a week the children come to the I. L. Peretz School, on Long Island, to learn Jewish history and culture. In 1973 I came to the school to register Nancy as a student, and become one of the teachers.

I love teaching the children, who know few Yiddish words, the language of their grandparents. I love bringing them closer to their heritage through songs, through stories.

"*Ayns*. One. *Tzway*. Two. *Dray*. Three." Slowly, clearly, I repeat the numbers in Yiddish, in English. "*Ayns. Tzway. Dray*," the kids repeat after me.

"Mrs. Sender." Nine-year-old Adam raises his hand. His big, dark eyes twinkle. His dark hair tossed over his forehead, a mischievous smile plays softly on his lips. "Mrs. Sender, would you please repeat *three?*"

"Okay, Adam. *Dray. Dray. Dray,*" I say slowly.

"I mean in English."

I try to hide my amusement. "Why? You speak English very well."

"Well, I like the way you say *three*." He grins brightly. "It sounds funny."

The kids stare at him, annoyed. "You are very rude." Eight-year-old Miriam, her light brown ponytail flying high as she stands up, scolds him. "Mrs. Sender is from another country, and some of her words sound a little different, Adam. So?"

I turn toward Miriam. "You are right."

On the blackboard I write *TH* in big, bold letters. "Some sounds, like *th*, are not part of the languages I spoke as a child."

"You spoke more than one language?" I hear someone gasp.

I nod. "Some English words sound different when spoken by people to whom English is not their first language." I stop. "That does not mean that we should make fun of the way these people speak."

Miriam, her eyes flashing, looks triumphantly at Adam.

"I'm sorry." Adam lowers his eyes. "I was just curious."

"It is good to be curious. If we are curious and ask questions, we learn."

My eyes move slowly over the bright faces before me. My daughter, Nancy, is one of my students. As our eyes meet, her lips whisper silently, "I love you."

"I come from a land called Poland."

"Where is Poland?" someone asks quickly.

"Far away, in Eastern Europe." I stop, take a deep breath. "A long time ago, children in a displaced persons camp in Germany—Jewish children, waiting for a place to call home—asked me, 'Where is America?' "

"I go to camp every year. It's fun," a happy voice cries out loudly.

I look at the window. "It was not that kind of a camp." I turn back to the class.

"What is a 'displaced person,' Mrs. Sender?" a child asks softly.

"A person who lost his or her home and has no place to go."

"That's sad." I hear a quiet comment. "It must be scary."

"Those children finally came to America?" a child asks hopefully.

"Some did. Some went to other faraway countries."

"What are the children doing in America now?"

I smile. "Those children are grown now. Most of them are professionals."

"My parents are professionals."

"Mine are, too."

I nod. The voices subside.

"Some of those children are married." I move about the front of the class as I speak. "Some have children of their own. My sons, Louie and Allen, are two of those children."

"Are they married?" asks a little girl, her short, red, curly hair forming a crown on her head.

"They both are. Louie's wife is named Judy and Allen's wife is Mindy."

"Do they have children?" the child continues.

"Do you have to know everything?" A boy in the back row hisses at her. "You're a busybody, Susan."

"Mrs. Sender said it's good to ask questions, Scott."

"You're still a busybody." Scott grimaces.

"Judy and Louie have two little girls, Jennifer and Amy. Mindy and Allen have a little boy named Eric. I have two granddaughters and a grandson."

My eyes well up with tears.

The children stare at me.

"Why are you crying?" I hear a bewildered voice.

"These are tears of joy." I smile as I wipe the tears from my face.

47

"Why, Mommy? Why? Why did the Nazis kill my grandparents?"

The question I knew Nancy would ask one day startles me. The pain in her eyes, the sadness in her voice are all too familiar. Louie. Allen. Harvey. Nancy. Each child asks the same painful question.

"The Nazis were evil."

"Why did they let them do it? Why didn't people stop them?"

I bite my lips. "Why did they let them do it?" I put my arms around her, hold her tight.

"But, Mommy, it couldn't happen here. Our neighbors, our friends, they would help."

Painful memories of betrayal rush through my mind. My childhood friends. My childhood neighbors. They did not help. Why?

Suddenly the gentle blue eyes of Antosha, our Christian housekeeper, appear before me. *I did not betray you.*

144

Antosha. Before I was born, she came to us, as a young woman, from a small village. We became her family. When my father died suddenly during a typhus epidemic, and Mama, with six young children, expecting the seventh, was left to raise them alone, Antosha was by her side even when Mama had no money to pay her wages. "Look for a family that can pay you, Antosha," Mama urged.

"You are my family," was the reply. "If you struggle, I will struggle."

She shopped carefully to save every cent she could to run the household while Mama ran the tailor shop. We were her children. Our home was her home.

Then the Nazis invaded. Antosha made trips to her village to bring back food. The Jews of Lodz were put into the ghetto and the order came for all non-Jews to leave the area. Antosha refused to leave us.

"Antosha. My dear Antosha," Mama pleaded with tears in her eyes. "Who knows what will happen to us? You must not stay. You have family to go to."

"No. You are my family. I will not leave you!" she cried.

"Antosha, the Germans may put you in prison. They may send you away to forced labor in Germany."

"I cannot leave. You are my family."

"You must go, my dear Antosha. It will not help us if they take you by force." Mama held her close. "Soon this will be over and you will come back to us. My children will come back. We will be a family again."

They held each other in a long, tight embrace. Mama did not survive. I never saw Antosha again.

"No, Antosha, you did not betray us," I whisper silently.

Tears glide over my face. Nancy wipes them away gently. *It couldn't happen here.* Nancy's words echo around me.

I see the warm, friendly faces of my present neighbors, and I wonder: What would they do? Would they close their eyes, their ears, their hearts? Would they risk their lives? Could it happen again?

You never speak about it. A neighbor's bewildered eyes are vivid in my mind.

You never speak about it. My son's words ring accusingly in my ears.

Tell about us. We died. You survived, the voices in my head urge.

But will they listen?

How will they learn? You must speak about the past!

But it is too hard. Too painful, I argue silently.

You must! command the voices. *You must!*

"Could it happen again?" Nancy asks. "Could it?"

"If we forget the past, it could happen again. We must learn from the past. We must learn what happens when people remain silent while others are persecuted."

Nancy puts her head in my lap. I stroke her hair gently. "As long as there is life, there is hope," I whisper.

48

"What are we doing today, Mrs. Sender?"

A group of ten- to twelve-year-old children fills the room. An array of dark, blond, brown, red hair. Blue eyes, brown eyes, dark eyes. A sea of warm colors glistening in the sun.

One child rests his head on the desk. Not all of them rise eagerly on a weekend to attend Jewish school. They would rather sleep late (I would, too). They could watch television, play with friends. Still, they are here.

I am happy to see them. I am happy to be with them. "Let's take out our last issue of *Jewish Current Events,* children." The swishing of newspaper, mixed with moans and groans, fills the room.

"Let's do the silly riddles," Jordan calls out, his blue eyes twinkling. "Where was Noah when evening came?"

"He was in d'ark," shouts Jason, tossing his light-brown hair away from his forehead.

"Children." My eyes move disapprovingly from Jordan to Jason. "Please raise your hands. You may each choose one item in the magazine that you want to read."

Hands pop up. Different magazine headlines are called out, some greeted with approval, some disapproval.

"Pilgrims found the idea for a Thanksgiving day in the Bible."

"Riddles."

"You can believe it!"

"World News."

"U.S. Nazis may have to leave."

I wait patiently to get their attention. "Well, I would like to discuss the 'What Do You Think?' questions."

Some children grimace.

I smile. "After you have read your choices. Let's start with the Thanksgiving topic, since we are about to celebrate Thanksgiving." I turn to Cindy, sitting in the last row. Her face lights up. "Cindy, that was your choice."

Cindy straightens her strawberry-blond hair quickly, as if preparing for a performance. " 'The Pilgrims—' " Her voice trembles nervously. She stops, begins again. Then she reads the article, which says that the Pilgrims may have gotten the idea for the Thanksgiving celebration from the biblical description of the Jewish holiday of Sukkoth. Toward the end, her voice takes on strength. " 'In coming to America, the early Pilgrims compared themselves with the Israelites. Just as the Israelites crossed the Red Sea to escape a cruel pharaoh in Egypt, so did the Pilgrims cross the Atlantic Ocean to escape from England.' "

Cindy takes a deep breath and sits down.

"We have many freedoms," I comment slowly. "Many freedoms we take for granted."

"You mean the freedom to study our heritage?"

"Freedom of speech."

"Freedom to travel from place to place."

I nod my head approvingly as the kids show their knowledge of freedoms.

The children take turns reading the articles they have chosen.

It is Jimmy's turn to read. He looks silently at me for a moment, then begins. " 'The United States finally is taking action against former Nazis who live in this country. It cannot punish them for their crimes, but it can send them out of the country for giving false information about themselves when they became American citizens.' "

The face of the American immigration official in Germany flashes before my eyes. *Were you a member of the Nazi party?* I hear the embarrassment in his voice as he questions Moniek and me. *I have to ask. Some Nazis pose as survivors to escape justice.*

" 'One of the accused was a former police official in Latvia,' " I hear Jimmy read. " 'He wore a Nazi uniform and selected Jews to be murdered. His idol was Adolf Hitler. He now lives in Long Island, a New York suburb.' "

The children wait silently for me to say something.

"It has taken a long time, but maybe if they are found and deported, they will stand trial in the countries where the crimes were committed."

Adam studies my face carefully. "Mrs. Sender, what good will it do now? It will not bring back those who died."

"You are right. It will not bring back the dead, but putting the Nazis on trial means that the world will hear of their crimes." I stop, take a deep breath. "And I hope the world will learn from it so that it can never happen again to any people."

I look at the clock on the classroom wall. "See you next week, children. No homework."

"Yippee!"

"Have a nice weekend," kids shout as they rush outside.

I place my books into my attaché case and turn to leave. A mother, her eyes flashing angrily, rushes toward me. "How dare you!"

I stare at her, bewildered.

"How dare you tell our kids stories that there are Nazis in Long Island?" she shouts. "I do not want you to teach my child about the Holocaust."

Cold sweat covers my body. A Jewish mother, in a Jewish school, objecting to the teaching of the Holocaust. Does she know how close she came to being one of the victims? But she does not want to hear. She does not want her child to know.

You must teach! You must teach! The voices of those who died call to me.

I take a deep breath. "The fact is that there *are* Nazis in Long Island, where we live, and in many other parts of the United States. Your child read it in a *Jewish Current Events* issue."

My heart pounds. "And about teaching the Holocaust. We must learn from the past to have a future. Knowledge does not hurt; ignorance does."

The tone of my voice startles her. She stares at me for a moment, turns, and walks angrily out of the classroom.

My legs tremble. I sit down, put my head on the table, and sob.

49

Will Jimmy show up? I wonder as I watch the children arriving for school. His mother contacted the school board after our painful confrontation last week. The board stood by me.

The children settle at their desks as the door opens slowly. Jimmy enters. His face is pale. His eyes red. He looks uncomfortable as he hands me a note. "I'm sorry I'm late," he whispers.

"I am glad to see you, Jimmy," I reply softly as he moves toward a desk.

I glance at the note. "Please forgive Jimmy for being late. I intended to keep him out, but he got very upset." I fold the note, put it on the desk, turn toward the class.

"Last week we spoke of freedoms." I move closer to my students. "I am glad that we live in a country of freedoms. I am free to choose what I teach. You are free to choose to learn."

I look at Jimmy. Our eyes meet. A gentle smile appears on his lips.

"When I was a child. . . ." I rest against the desk. Eyes light up. They love my "when I was a child" stories. "When I was in school in Poland, we learned a poem about freedom." I stop. "I told you about this poem, didn't I?"

"Tell us again," a child prompts.

"Well. A famous Polish poet compared freedom to good health. We only value it when we have lost it."

"That means we should value freedom," another child comments.

"What was your school like?"

"Were you a good student?"

"What did you do after school?"

"Tell us about your teachers."

"Did you like your teachers?"

I close my eyes for a moment. "I was a very quiet student. I only answered questions when the teacher called on me."

"Just like me." Brian's face lights up. "I don't like to raise my hand."

"Me, too." Melissa smiles. "I'm always afraid that I'll sound dumb."

Other kids nod in silent agreement.

"No one is dumb. We just need a little confidence," I assure them. The faces of my teachers flash before my eyes. "My teachers helped me a lot." I smile. "One of my teachers was my Uncle Baruch. He taught science, math, art, and gym. Everybody loved him."

"Did you call him Uncle at school?"

"No. I called him Teacher." My fingers lace tightly together. "I had wonderful teachers. There was Mr. Melman, my history teacher. Always serious. From behind his heavy glasses his eyes had a gentle, special smile. And there was Mrs. Melman, his wife, pretty, with warm, smiling eyes. She taught Yiddish, Yiddish literature. They had a son, Baynish. He would sit in the classroom—he was too young for school—and ask many questions."

"Did he call them Mom and Dad, Mrs. Sender?"

I see the dark, curly head, the inquisitive eyes. I hear his childish voice. *Teacher, I have a question.*

I sigh softly. "No. He addressed them as Teacher."

"It must be neat to have both of your parents in school," one child comments.

"Well, if you get into trouble, they know right away," another proclaims.

I nod. "And there was Miss Winograd, who taught geography. She was great. She traveled a lot and would show us pictures of the places she visited, tell about the foods, the customs of those faraway places. We all loved it."

I stop. I see Miss Winograd, her short, dark hair combed smoothly toward her face, standing in front of a map, pointing. *This is where I was.*

"Miss Yoskowicz taught Polish and Polish literature and always told many stories of when she was a child in school."

"Just like you," Jordan calls.

"Just like me."

"What did she look like?"

"Tell us some of her stories, please."

"She was tall, blond, always happy. Her voice had a musical tone. She loved to tell stories with a message."

"You mean learning stories, like you do," Paul remarks.

I nod as I continue. "A boy had not done his homework.

" 'Tell the teacher that you will make it up,' said his mother.

" 'My teacher will not know. I can get away with it,' he bragged.

" 'Your teacher will know when she looks at you that you did not do your homework.'

"He looked at her, smiling. 'No, she will not.'

" 'She will, too,' the mother insisted. 'It will be written on your forehead with invisible ink. Teachers can read invisible writing.'

"The child left for school thinking, Maybe Mommy is right. He rubbed his forehead hard, just in case. His forehead turned real red. He entered the classroom.

"The teacher noticed his red forehead. 'What is this I see?' she asked, concerned.

" 'Mommy was right!' the child shouted. 'It is written that I did not do my homework.'

"The teacher, trying to hide her amusement, answered seriously, 'Teachers can read invisible writing. So you may as well tell the truth.' "

"Mrs. Sender," Cindy asks bashfully, "can teachers really read children's faces?"

"My mother says the teachers have eyes in the back of their heads!" Jimmy calls out.

155

The children burst out laughing.

"Teachers can do many, many things." My eyes glide slowly over the faces of the children.

The laughter stops. "What happened to your teachers?" Paul asks.

I feel a stabbing pain in my chest. "They all perished." The children stare silently at me.

"Does it hurt to talk about them?" Cindy asks.

"It hurts to talk about them." I clear my voice. "But when I talk to you about them, you, too, get to know them and their stories. Their wisdom lives on. We learn from the past."

"I like when you talk about your childhood, Mrs. Sender."

Paul looks around the classroom. "People in different countries are not so different. Maybe we have more stuff."

"Very well put, Paul." I smile broadly. "Very well put."

"You should put your stories in a book. I mean the ones about your family." Jordan moves away from his desk as he speaks. "Other people should learn from your stories, too."

"He's right."

"You should."

"You should."

"That's what my children keep telling me. Maybe someday. . . ."

50

Other people should learn. I hear the children's voices as I write of family love amid degradation. Compassion amid selfishness. Spiritual resistance amid horror and death.

I mail my story to *World Over*, a magazine for young people published by the Board of Jewish Education in New York. Maybe they will find it worth publishing. Maybe. . . .

Two years ago, in 1974, an anti-Semitic remark made by an American general shook me up. What happened during the Holocaust could happen again, here, I thought. I wrote an episode of my life and sent it to *Newsday*. John Pascal, a *Newsday* columnist, wrote a piece entitled, "It Can Happen Here." He included my story, giving me full credit. The story had a strong impact.

Within a few days, an envelope arrives from *World Over*. It is a skinny envelope. I hold my breath. That means they did not return the story, or it would be bulky. My hands tremble as I open it.

Dear Mrs. Sender:
Thank you very much for sending us your moving story. We hope to use it in our Yom

157

Hashoah (Holocaust Remembrance Day) issue
this year.

Best wishes,

Ezekiel Schloss

Editor

I read the short letter again and again. They want my story. They want to remember.

I see the faces of my little brothers, Motele, Laibele, Moishele. I feel their presence as I write another piece for *World Over*. "Can the children, the adults in America identify with names sounding strange to their ears? Names they cannot pronounce?" I wonder aloud. "Maybe if I Americanize the names of my brothers, they will become *their* brothers, *their* children."

In *Hadassah* magazine I used Americanized names: Mark for Motele, Leon for Laibele, Murray for Moishele. But when I read the piece, it seems as though I am speaking of someone else, not my little brothers. "Still"—I argue with myself—"you are writing so that others can identify with your family. To you they will always be your brothers, no matter what names you use."

A reply to my new piece comes within days, again from the editor of *World Over, * Ezekiel Schloss.

Dear Mrs. Sender:

We are happy to tell you that we are accepting your story for publication, but we do have a few questions. We feel that it would add realism if you called your brothers by their Yiddish names. What were they called at home?

Also, do you have any photographs of yourself and/or your brothers at about the age the story takes place? We may not actually use the photographs, but they would be an excellent guide for our illustrator.

I read the letter through tear-blurred eyes. Thank you, Mr. Schloss, for helping me resolve my inner struggle.

Photographs? I blink away my tears. I wish I had photographs. I gaze at the picture of my brother Laibele, taken in school before the Holocaust. The picture, which hangs over my desk, was found by some survivors in the garbage of my home after liberation. These people remembered the secret library at our home. They went to salvage the books. They found them in the garbage in the yard, thrown there by the Polish family who had taken over our home. In the garbage were also photographs of my Uncle Baruch, their teacher. They gave us the photographs. Among them was a photograph of Laibele.

My father's sister, from Argentina, sent us a picture of my parents and a group picture of my parents, Mama's parents, her two brothers, a sister-in-law, and my sisters as children. Those are the only pictures left of my family.

I wish I had photographs.

51

"My students read your stories. They are touched. You were about their age during the Holocaust."

I listen nervously to the man on the telephone. He is the principal of the Hebrew school in Long Island.

"Would it be possible for you to come to our school? It would mean a lot to our students. Please."

My heart beats fast. It is the first time I am asked to speak to a group other than my own students. I hesitate for a moment.

"The kids are eager to meet you, Mrs. Sender. Please say yes."

"I will be there." I try to sound calm as we set a date.

He greets me warmly when I arrive at the school. On the floor in his office is a stack of *World Over* magazines. I recognize the issue on top. It has one of my stories.

I feel overwhelmed. Is this real? Children in a school reading my stories?

"The students are so excited about your visit." He, too, appears nervous as he leads me to the sanctuary of the synagogue, next door to the Hebrew school.

"This is Ruth Minsky Sender, the author of the moving stories we read."

I watch the children's faces as I am being introduced.

Their eyes are filled with wonder. I must keep myself from shaking. I lean on the podium for support.

"My Yiddish name is Riva. I am a Holocaust survivor." I see them studying my face, my hair, my clothing.

"She's the girl in the stories," someone whispers from the front row.

"I know you have read my stories in *World Over*. Some of you may even have read my stories in *Hadassah* magazine and *Newsday*."

Some kids nod.

"I'll tell you a little about myself and then let you ask questions. I hope I have answers."

I speak of childhood in Poland. Of persecution. Of hunger. Of the will to survive. Not a sound is heard. All eyes are on my face. My voice trembles from time to time. I gaze at my watch. It has been more than one hour. Still the children listen silently.

"We must learn from the past to have a future." I take a deep breath. "Thank you for listening. Now please ask questions."

Silence hangs heavily in the sanctuary.

"I know there are many questions. Some are hard to ask." I move closer to the students. "I am sure you heard of the wisdom of Rabbi Hillel. He lived a long time ago. He said, 'A bashful person cannot learn. Nor can an irritable person teach.' If you are too bashful to ask questions, you will never learn. If you are too impatient to answer questions, you should not be a teacher." I try to smile. "I have lots of patience; please ask questions."

Slowly hands are raised. "Did you ever find your brothers Motele and Moishele?" a child asks softly. He says their names naturally, easily. They are people he feels close to.

I shake my head.

"Are your stories true?"

"How did you feel when your neighbors betrayed you?"

"Would you ever go back to Poland or Germany?"

"What helped you survive?"

"What happened to your cousin Sabcia?"

"Do you hate Germans?"

"Do you have nightmares?"

"Did you ever want to give up?"

Questions flow. My voice breaks as I answer each question.

"Do you often speak to your sons and your daughter about the past?" a teacher asks.

"It is not a topic one speaks about at the dinner table. It is too painful for them. It is too painful for me."

A boy wearing a baseball hat stands up. "It's obviously hard for you to speak about this. You're trying not to cry." His eyes are on my face. "Why do it?"

"It is hard, very hard for me to control my emotions. But"—I clear my throat—"I do not want pity. None of the survivors want pity. We want you to learn from our painful past so that it can never happen again. You must never forget."

We will remember, their eyes assure me. We will.

"Thank you."

Applause echoes loudly around me. Children encircle me. Arms reach out to touch me, to hug me.

"Thank you for sharing," a girl whispers. "When I read your stories, I felt as if I were there with you."

I hug her silently.

52

With each personal appearance at public schools, private schools, temples, parochial schools, organizations, I gain more confidence. In each new published piece, I share more of the past. I feel drained each time I walk away from the typewriter.

"Mrs. Sender, I am Mr. Irvin, Nancy's social studies teacher at Sawmill Junior High," a man introduces himself over the telephone.

"Is there a problem with Nancy?" I ask nervously.

"Oh, no. I wish I had many students like Nancy."

"Thank you." I smile, pleased with his comment. I remember hearing the same remarks from Louie's teachers, Allen's teachers, Harvey's teachers.

"The reason I am calling—" he stops. "I read your poignant stories in *Newsday*." He hesitates for a moment. "I hate to impose, but I need you. My students need you." His voice shakes slightly. "If you speak as you write. . . ." He stops again.

It is Nancy's class. How will she feel? Thoughts rush quickly through my mind as I listen to his request.

"Our children study World War II, but there are only a few lines in our textbooks about the Holocaust. I am searching for ways to supplement their knowledge."

"I will be there," I answer quickly.

We set a date.

Will Nancy be upset? How will her classmates react on learning that she is a child of Holocaust survivors? Will I cause her pain? Maybe I should not go.

The hands of my kitchen clock move slowly as I wait for Nancy to return from school.

"Mr. Irvin told our social studies class that you will speak to us about your childhood." Nancy puts down her books, puts her arms around me. "He told the class that you're a teacher, a writer, a Holocaust survivor, but he didn't say that you're my mother. Some of the kids looked in my direction when they heard the name Sender."

"Will it make you uncomfortable? The kids do not know that your parents are Holocaust survivors."

"I never speak about that." She holds me tight. "I know it's important that they learn from you. They don't know anything about the Holocaust. I'll be all right, Mom. I'll be all right."

I swallow the lump in my throat.

53

I enter Nancy's classroom, escorted by her teacher. All eyes are on me. The assistant principal, Mrs. Argus, sits in the back of the room. She greets me with a warm smile.

I search for Nancy. My heart beats fast as our eyes meet in silent understanding.

The students have photocopies of my *Newsday* articles on their desks. (I have now been published in *Newsday* several times.) *They don't know anything about the Holocaust.* Again I hear Nancy's remark.

"Now they know a little," a small voice within me whispers. "And they will learn more."

They listen intently, silently as I speak. I try hard to control my emotions. It is your child you are speaking to, the little voice within me keeps whispering.

"It is important that you learn what hatred, prejudice, and indifference can lead to. At a time when there are still living witnesses to the Holocaust, some people try to deny that it happened."

"I just received that kind of literature," Mr. Irvin calls out angrily. "It was mailed to me as the chairman of social studies at this school. I threw it in the garbage, where it belongs."

He rushes to the wastebasket, pulls out a journal, and hands it to me. "It's published in California by a group called the Institute of Historical Review. With this"—he looks in disgust at the publication—"came a letter. They want me to advise my teachers to teach that the Holocaust never happened."

Mrs. Argus gasps. "They sent this to our school?"

I shiver as I hold the journal. "I saw how hatred and prejudice can be taught. We must not allow it. Remember that you must stand guard against it. The Holocaust did happen. My family perished. Remember."

Mrs. Argus rushes toward me. She puts her arms around me. "I'm sorry," she whispers through tears. "I'm so sorry."

The students leave the classroom quietly. Nancy looks in my direction. Her lips move silently: "I love you."

I watch Nancy's school bus stop at the corner. I wait in front of the house for her. "Are you okay?" I ask.

She nods. "Mrs. Argus spoke about you during an assembly. She told the students that you're my mother and that she is proud to have met you. Some of the kids looked at me strangely, as if they didn't really know me."

She takes my hand in hers. "I'm proud that you're my mother."

I pull her close to me. "I am proud that you are my daughter."

54

"Moniek. April 1983 will be forty years since the Warsaw ghetto uprising." I look from the letter in my hands toward Moniek. "To commemorate the fortieth anniversary, there will be an American gathering of Jewish Holocaust survivors, their children, and their grandchildren in Washington, D.C., April 11 to 14."

A dark cloud covers his face. "What do we need a gathering for? The dead will not return." Bitterness and anger shout from his eyes.

"It is for the survivors. Look at the emblem."

We stare silently at the two intertwined round links. Inside one is a flame. Beside it, in Hebrew, Yiddish, and English, "Remember. 6,000,000." Inside the other is a ripped-open barbed wire Star of David. From the open edges of the barbed wire blossom new leaves. In the center large letters proclaim boldly:

TOGETHER

FROM HOLOCAUST

TO NEW LIFE!

"Together from Holocaust to new life," I repeat, fighting back tears.

"My parents, my brothers will not be there." Moniek's voice breaks.

"But . . . maybe . . . maybe somehow. . . ." I speak softly. "Maybe someone did survive. Or maybe we'll find someone who saw, heard—"

"You are a dreamer." He raises his voice. "If we did not find anyone or hear anything before now. . . . You wrote to organizations in Poland, Switzerland, Israel. No one is to be found. You wrote to Polish town halls. No trace. Swallowed by the earth. What are you searching for?"

"You, too, sometimes wonder. . . ." I try to defend my fruitless efforts. "Maybe . . . at the gathering. . . ."

"I am not going." He stares at the kitchen window. "I have no reason to go."

"You may be right, Moniek. Still I want to go."

"You are crazy!"

"I will ask Nancy to come with me."

"Do what you want," he mumbles angrily.

"I am sure my sisters, Mala and Chana, will go. Chana may bring her Susan."

"You are all crazy."

"If I do not go, I will always wonder if I could have found someone."

He shrugs his shoulders.

"I understand how you feel, Moniek. But I must go."

He walks angrily out of the kitchen.

55

The Capital Centre, the location of the gathering, is officially named Survivors' Village for the three-day event. Survivors and their children crowd around walls plastered with notes.

"Did you see my family?"

"Did you ever hear this name?"

"Before the war I lived in. . . ."

Names. Addresses. Only the names, the places differ. The questions are the same. Eyes search eagerly, hopefully. Hearts pound. Maybe. . . . Heavy, painful sighs of failure, frustration fill the air.

Faces of the first survivors I met, after liberation from the concentration camps, on the roads in Germany flash before me. I see their searching eyes. I hear names. I hear addresses. I hear their desperate questions.

Have you seen . . . ?

Have you heard . . . ?

I feel tightness in my chest. Tears sting my eyes. We are all here for the same reason.

You are a dreamer. I hear Moniek's voice.

All of us here are dreamers. Hoping. . . .

You all are crazy. Moniek's angry words spin in my head.

Maybe we are. We are living with false hope.

Long lines to the computers, attempting to match names, places, dates. Long lines to the microphone open to the survivors. Quivering, pleading voices.

"My name is . . ."

"I am from . . ."

"Have you seen . . . ?"

"Have you heard . . . ?"

We are searching. Forever searching.

56

Each person at the gathering wears a name tag. My name tag reads: Ruth Sender, Commack, NY. Riva Minska, Lodz.

Carefully, eagerly, I search people's faces. Do they resemble someone I once knew? Do those eyes look familiar? I move closer, read their tags.

"Mom, it's not nice to bend so close to people," Nancy comments, embarrassed by my behavior. "What will they think?"

"My child, today I do not care about manners. I cannot read the tags otherwise."

She takes my hand in hers. Quickly her eyes move from tag to tag to tag, and she reads names, places aloud.

Sometimes an outcry of joy rings out. Someone has found a childhood friend, an old schoolmate. Newsmen rush to record the few reunions.

A man looks at my tag. Looks at my face.

"Riva Minska." He repeats my name slowly. "I used to take books from your secret library in the ghetto."

"It was not my library, it was our library," I hasten to correct him as I read his name tag.

"Levin, I remember you. You had a younger sister."

He nods slowly. He is about to ask something, but the

question remains frozen on his lips. We stare at each other. I read the unspoken question in his pain-filled eyes: Your brothers? Did they survive? I shake my head.

"My little sister," he whispers hoarsely. "My little sister, also gone."

Tears glisten in his eyes. Tears flow over my cheeks. He puts his arms around me. "We must be strong, Riva."

I press him close to me. "We must be strong," I whisper as we part to go on with our fruitless search.

My eyes dart from face to face, probing, searching.

"This is my son and my two grandchildren." A woman before me proudly presents her family to someone. "We survived to build a new life."

Before my eyes flash the joy-filled faces of two people at last night's opening ceremony of the American Gathering of Jewish Holocaust Survivors. Rabbi Herschel Schacter of the Bronx, NY, a former chaplain of the US Army, and Rabbi Israel Lou of Netanya, Israel.

"April 11, 1945, I was with the American army that liberated the Buchenwald concentration camp." Rabbi Schacter addresses the gathering, his arms around Rabbi Lou. "I saw piles of corpses." His voice cracks. "Among the piles of corpses I saw the petrified eyes of a seven-year-old boy, staring at me. He was still alive."

He stops, holds tight to Rabbi Lou. "This is the child I discovered alive in a pile of death." Tears flow over his face. "The child who defied death, a spiritual leader of his people. Rabbi Israel Lou."

I look around me. All of us here defied death. Some rose to very prominent positions in law, medicine, education, literature, art, the business world.

I feel a sudden wave of joy. We are here. Survivors. Children. Grandchildren. From Holocaust to new life.

57

A section of the Survivors' Village houses exhibitions of art by Holocaust survivors. Paintings, poems, songs, depicting the past, bringing hope for the future, call to me from the walls, from the tables. I stare in awe at the talent that survived destruction and found the physical and spiritual strength to create again.

I stop at a publisher's booth. I use their textbooks in my classes to teach Jewish history, moral values, personalities whose important contributions made a difference to humanity.

Could I make a difference? My heart beats faster. "I have a manuscript at home titled *The Cage*. I hope to publish it." I feel nervous as I address the middle-aged man leaning against the table laden with books on Jewish topics.

He smiles. His eyes wander curiously over my face. "Publishing is not easy."

"I do not know anything about publishing," I comment softly.

"What is *The Cage* about?" He slowly straightens the books on the table.

"I am a Holocaust survivor." My voice quivers slightly. "I was a child. One of the children who survived. I wrote about my little brothers. They did not survive. I wrote of spiritual resistance. I hope the world will learn from it."

"My dear lady." His voice is low. "Who wants to read about the Holocaust?"

His comment, spoken so matter-of-factly, fills me with horror.

"Everyone, young and old, should read." I raise my voice.

"You are right. But as a publisher, I know that Holocaust books do not sell." He sighs. "It is a bad investment."

"But we must remember. We must remember." The words choke me. "We must remember the past so that it can never happen again."

He fumbles with some papers before him. "My dear lady, it is a sad fact that Holocaust books do not sell." He repeats his heartbreaking statement. "Do you have children? Grandchildren?" His eyes suddenly brighten.

I nod, puzzled.

"Well, then. Take your manuscript to a printer, make photocopies for your children, your grandchildren, and forget about publishing."

My heart beats fast. I stare speechlessly at the man before me.

"I'm sorry." He avoids my eyes.

"I will not give up." My voice sounds strange. "I will not give up."

58

June 1985. I read the letter again and again as I blink away my tears.

Dear Mrs. Sender:

I am writing on behalf of Macmillan's Children's Book Department to say that we have read your manuscript entitled *The Cage* and are interested in publishing it. Our reason is not only that the story is true and grippingly told, but also that it is a remarkable testament to human fortitude and faith in the face of unspeakable evil.

It is your strength to survive, then, your wish to live and flourish in spite of this experience, that gives the story its deepest value. It is this, too, that makes it possible for the reader to endure one horrifying episode after another. . . .

My tears flow over my face. I read the last paragraph aloud.

In closing I would like to state the obvious, that I am deeply impressed with your manuscript, which in and of itself is an act of rare personal courage. It would be a privilege to work with you.

Thank you for sending your manuscript to us, and

All the best,

Sincerely,
Beverly Reingold
Senior Editor

Nervously, I dial the phone number given in the letter. "This is Ruth Minsky Sender." My voice quivers.

"I'm Beverly Reingold. I'm so glad to hear from you."
The warmth in her voice puts me at ease. "Thank you.
I am overwhelmed by your letter." I clear my throat. "I
am glad that I did not give up hope."

"Macmillan will be honored to publish your work. I
would love to meet you face to face. Let's have lunch."
She stops for a moment. "Ever since I read your moving
manuscript, I have the overwhelming desire to feed you,
to see you eat, to know that you're not hungry."

"I will never forget the pain of hunger." I sigh. "After
all the years of starvation, free to eat as much as I want.
Now I worry about gaining weight."

"We all do." I hear a soft chuckle. "I still want to feed
you."

"It is strange, Beverly, but I feel like I know you."

"I feel that way, too, Ruth."

We speak for a long time. I hold the phone in my
trembling hands. Dazed, I stare at the only picture of my
little brother Laibele. "My book is becoming a reality," I
whisper.

His gentle eyes smile softly, approvingly at me.

59

"Mrs. Sender? Ruth Minsky Sender? The author of *The Cage?*" the woman on the telephone inquires nervously.

"Yes. I am Ruth Minsky Sender, the author of *The Cage.*"

"I'm sorry if I'm imposing."

"You are not imposing."

"Mrs. Sender, I am so excited to have located you. I'm Cindy, a teacher in a middle school in Tulare, California. My students and I read *The Cage.* We are all so touched by it. We are moved by your experiences and the way you share them."

The words rush from her mouth. "I never saw those kids so eager to read a book. I saw on the jacket of the book that you live in Commack, New York. So I called information." She takes a deep breath. "I'm so happy to have this chance to speak to you. The kids would love to write to you, if it's okay. They have so many, many questions."

"I am overwhelmed that my story has had such a strong impact. I will gladly answer their questions. I receive many letters. I always answer them."

"I am sure the readers appreciate hearing from you."

"If they take the time to write, the least I can do is answer."

"Do you know where we are in California?" Her voice is low. "We are in an area where the neo-Nazis peddle their ugly propaganda that the Holocaust never happened." There is pain and anger in her voice.

"I am familiar with their horrifying literature. It scares me."

"We, the teachers around here, are teaching the Holocaust through your book. Our students learn from it what hatred and prejudice lead to."

Tears glide over my face.

"I spoke to the other teachers about *The Cage*. They all tell me that students who never picked up a book to read for pleasure didn't want to stop reading. Some of the kids asked to stay after school and read so that they could find out what happened next. We are all learning so much."

She takes an audible breath. "I cannot find enough words to describe what that book means to us. We can never repay the debt."

I hear the voice of the publisher at the gathering of Holocaust survivors. *Who wants to read about the Holocaust?*

I swallow hard. "I cannot find enough words to describe how I feel at the moment. How much your call means to me."

"My colleagues and my students will not believe that I spoke to you." She chuckles. "I can't believe it."

"Do you need a note for the teacher?" I smile.

She laughs. I hear music in her laughter. I hear Mama's voice. *As long as there is life, there is hope.*

60

Letters from Tulare arrive shortly. I stare in amazement at the hundreds of letters before me, written by young adults, written by teachers.

Dear Riva,

I hope that you don't mind the children calling you Riva. We've used your name throughout the story and you seem so familiar to us. All the seventh-grade students have read your book in Tulare City School District, approximately six hundred students a year. We teach values, issues, caring, prejudice, family relationships, and so much more surrounding your book.

I have grown in knowledge and personally by reading your book. I look at my two children and wonder how and why the world could let this happen.

I read the teacher's words again and again. "I wonder how and why the world could let this happen." In my ears ring Mama's words. *A world full of people will not be silent.* I read letter after letter. My eyes fill with tears.

"How did you find the strength to live?"

"Are you really the girl in the book?"

"It is so hard to believe that something like that could happen."

"How did you feel when your German friends betrayed you?"

"Did you find your brothers?"

"How can people be so cruel to one another?"

"Did you ever think of giving up?"

"Do you still have nightmares?"

"How did it feel to finally be free?"

"I am glad that you survived to tell this story."

"I asked many times about the Holocaust and the answer was: 'It was terrible.' But you took me by the hand and I walked with you through the horrors. I shared your pain. I felt your love toward your family, your hope for tomorrow."

"I will never forget that the Holocaust did happen."

"The children loved your poem, 'Why?' written in a concentration camp. It left a very strong impact. They made up their own 'Why?' poems. They did artwork in response to your book."

Before me are large, brown envelopes filled with sensitive letters. Moving poems. Poems of anger, poems of hope. Artwork depicting scenes from *The Cage*.

Each poem, each letter, each picture is an outcry of anger, a message of hope.

"We will remember."

"We must not let it happen again to any people."

A poem that speaks of hope ends with the words, *As long as there is life, there is hope.* Mama's message of hope lives on.

61

One hundred fifty junior-high students at Sacred Heart School sit silently in front of me. The children each hold copies of *The Cage,* which they read in class. I feel their eyes on me.

"She is real."

"This is Riva."

"Her story is true."

"It did happen."

"Yes, it did happen." My voice, trembling at times, echoes in the stillness of the large hall.

The students raise their hands to ask questions, make comments. "I could never survive," a young girl says. "Where did you find the strength?"

"You do not know what you can or cannot survive until put to the test, child. We have more strength than we think we do."

"Did you ever think of ending it all?" another student asks.

"Yes. Each one of us did, at one time or another. But"—my voice takes on strength—"it took more courage to live than to give up."

I take a deep breath. "A girl in one of the concentration camps I was in tried to commit suicide. We were all angry at her because she was giving up. She survived. She lived to see freedom."

A boy with dark, curly hair stands up. "I thought people who went through that experience would be crazy, would have lost their minds." He stares at me. "It's amazing."

"It is amazing." I echo his words. "Many times we, the survivors, wonder why we are not crazy."

Sister Margaret, the principal, walks up and stands beside me. In her hand she holds an orange. She looks at me with tears in her eyes. "This morning, as I was about to fix my lunch for work, I put my hand in the refrigerator to take out an orange. I stopped. I remembered the scene in your book, when your little brothers sold their ration of bread to get one tangerine on the black market. They hoped that it would cure your malnutrition and make you able to walk again."

She puts the orange in my hand. "I know this orange comes much, much too late to help. It is only to show that I care."

My eyes well up with tears. "I understand," I whisper as we hold each other in a warm embrace.

The students gather around to have their books autographed.

I write, "As long as there is life, there is hope."

John Woods, a reporter from *The Tablet,* a Catholic newspaper, speaks to the children, writes down their reactions. He stops near Moniek, asks him something. Moniek's face turns pale. I hear the reporter softly apologizing.

"What happened, Moniek?" I ask as we are on our way home. "Why did the reporter apologize?"

Moniek remains silent. I wait for an answer.

"He wanted to know about Auschwitz. It was a natural question to ask when he saw the number on my arm." Moniek's voice cracks. "But I could not handle it. I choke. The words remain in my throat. Tears fill my eyes. He did not mean to upset me."

"He, too, looked upset, Moniek."

We drive in silence for a while.

"I wonder how you are able to do it." Moniek breaks the silence. "I know it is hard on you." He stops for a moment. "So why? Why do you need the nightmares that follow?"

"Moniek. We live with nightmares if we speak about

it or not." I feel the tightness in my throat. "Maybe by sharing our nightmares, I can make a difference."

He shrugs his shoulders.

"Maybe. . . ." I whisper, touching his arm softly.

We travel in silence.

What happened after liberation? Did someone take you on a plane and bring you to America? A question asked earlier echoes in my ears.

Later that day I speak to Harvey, repeating the question asked by the child.

"Mom, why don't you write about the displaced persons camps? We, your children, know so little about this."

I speak to Beverly Reingold, the editor of *The Cage.* "There is a story there, Ruth. Write it."

To Life. The book, about the survivors' struggle to find a home, to build a new life, is written.

62

"I am a Holocaust survivor." The woman's voice on the telephone trembles. "I am not from Lodz. I am from a small town in Poland. I am sure you do not know me." The words rush from her mouth nervously. "I must tell you that your books, *The Cage* and *To Life,* speak for all the survivors. Your story is our story. The names, the places change. The pain, the horrors remain the same." She sighs deeply. I hear in her sigh the collective outcry of pain of all the survivors. "I bought the books for my children. I could never speak to them about it."

"I understand."

For a moment there is silence.

"Thank you for having the courage and the ability to do it." She has changed from speaking English to Yiddish. "May you have the strength to continue. God bless you."

The same sentiments are expressed in the many Yiddish letters I receive from other Holocaust survivors.

"We give the books to our children."

"We give the books to our grandchildren."

"We must not forget."

"We must bear witness."

"Be strong."

"Tell the world."

The letters are also filled with questions.

"Did you ever meet someone by this name?"

"How do I search for my lost family?"

Forever searching. Fruitless searching. I wish at least once I could say, "Yes, I met them. Yes, they survived."

How could so many people vanish without a trace? I gaze at my books: *The Cage.* In hardcover and in paperback. In Dutch translation. In Danish translation. *To*

Life. Hardcover and paperback. In Danish translation. The books stare back at me with the agonizing eyes of those who perished, with the pain-filled eyes of those who survived. *Remember. Remember,* they call silently. My fingers move gently over each book. I feel the presence of my loved ones as I touch the books.

I look at the Dutch edition of *The Cage.* "Riva Minska. Number 55082." My eyes well up with tears.

Forget your names!

You must forget your names, you stupid cows!

Remember your numbers!

You must remember your numbers!

The vicious voices of the Nazi concentration camp guards still echo within me. The sound of their whips is all around me.

This is to make you remember your number!

This is to make you forget your name!

I blink away the tears, hold the book tightly in my hands. "Number 55082 survived. Riva Minska survived," I whisper.

Forget your name, the Nazi commandant's voice shouts in my ears.

"My name is Riva Minska. I survived."

You will have to tell our story. Voices of shriveled up young girls, ragged clothes hanging off their bony skeletons, pound in my head. *You will have to tell the world.*

Tell the world! call the voices of the survivors.

"We must learn from the past to have a future," whisper my trembling lips. I close my eyes. Mama's gentle face appears before me. *As long as there is life, there is hope.*

63

We give the books to our grandchildren. The words spin in my head as the faces of my grandchildren smile from pictures all over my house.

My older grandchildren, Jennifer, Amy, Eric, read my books. The younger ones, Ben, Brian, Matthew, Katie, are too young. My grandchildren. My heart fills with joy. My eyes glide lovingly over their faces.

Jennifer and Amy listen silently as I speak at their schools. "I'm proud that you're my grandmother," Jennifer whispers as she holds me tight, kisses me.

Around us are the students of the high-school Holocaust class I have shared my painful past with. The students watch with tears in their eyes. They, too, feel the miracle. A Holocaust survivor holding in her arms a grandchild. A third generation of survivors.

"My friends read your books, Grandma." Amy's blue eyes glow happily as I walk into her house. "They don't believe that you're my grandma."

"Well, next time I come to your junior high school, Amy, I'll make an announcement that you are my granddaughter and that I am proud of you."

"I'm proud of you, too, Grandma." She puts her arms around me. "I love you."

"I'm glad you survived to be my grandma." Ten-year-old Eric phones from his home in Georgia. "I learned a lot from your story. I love you."

Someday, when my younger grandchildren are old enough, they, too, will read my books. They, too, will learn of the world that vanished. The world of their grandparents' childhood.

Ben's puzzled blue eyes flash vividly before me. In my ears rings his distressed young voice as he stares at the blue concentration camp number on Moniek's arm. "Who put that number on your arm, Grandpa?"

Moniek seems uncomfortable. He looks away.

"Who put that number on your arm, Grandpa?" the child persists.

"Tell him, Dad." Harvey looks from the curiosity-filled eyes of his five-year-old son to the pain-filled eyes of his father. "Please answer him, Dad."

"Bad people put that number on my arm."

"Why, Grandpa?"

Why? I hear the voices of my children.

Why? I hear the voices of my grandchildren.

My heart beats fast. The child waits for an answer.

Moniek's lips tighten.

"Because they were mean, bad people, Grandpa?" Ben voices his opinion.

Moniek nods silently.

"Not all people are mean. Right, Dad?" Ben looks at his father for reassurance.

"There are many good people, Ben." Harvey puts his arms around him. "Not all people are bad."

64

August 1989. The sanctuary of Kehillat Chaim, Congregation of Life Synagogue, in Roswell, Georgia, is filled with smiling, festive people, gathered from many places to celebrate Eric's Bar Mitzvah, the coming of age of a Jewish child.

I look around. Next to me is Moniek. In the other pews are Louie, Judy, and their children, Jennifer and Amy. Harvey, Joanne, and their children, Ben and Katie, sit nearby. Nancy sits next to them. In the front pew sit Allen, Mindy, and their children, Eric, Brian, Matthew.

My heart sings. Our children. Our grandchildren. A congregation of life.

I gaze at Moniek. We defied death. Rose from the

ashes. Rebuilt a new life. Here we are. Proud parents. Happy grandparents. My family together in joy.

I close my eyes. Faces of loved ones who perished float slowly by. They, too, are with me. If only they had lived to share my joy.

"The Holocaust Lady." I remember the title given to me by a young child. "The Holocaust Lady." Her past, her present are intertwined.

Eric stands proudly at the lectern. He looks sure of himself as he reads his *haftarah,* a lesson from the Prophets.

Finished, he sighs a sigh of relief, looks with satisfaction at the people in the sanctuary. "I was asked today to summarize my feelings about becoming a bar mitzvah, a son of the commandments. Though I could probably write a book longer than my grandmother's, I hope you will gain some insight into the meaning of this day for me."

He speaks about book knowledge. Spiritual knowledge. Respect. Understanding one's heritage. Freedom to practice one's religion. The joy of grandparents, aunts, uncles, cousins sharing this day.

His words are music to my ears.

"To Grandma Ruth and Grandpa Morris: The significance of this day to the both of you cannot be described in words alone."

Tears well up in my eyes.

"I am the grandson of Holocaust survivors. I am a third

generation of Jews, which was never supposed to happen. If not for my grandparents' courage and faith, I would not be standing at this pulpit today."

He looks straight at us. "So with great love and admiration, I give this day to you."

Moniek is sobbing. I take his hand in mine, press it hard. I hear sobbing from the pews around me. My head is spinning.

Eric speaks of his parents, their love, the passing on of values, tradition. "I promise to pass down to my children someday what you taught me, Mom and Dad. I understand what I am and who I am. I am a Jew!"

I smile through my tears. "As long as there is life, there is hope, Mama," I whisper softly. "As long as there is life. . . ."